What Makes You So Strong?

Sermons of Joy and Strength from Jeremiah A. Wright, Jr.

To Delores
Stay Strong in the Lord!
J. Wright

What Makes You So Strong?

Sermons of Joy and Strength from Jeremiah A. Wright, Jr.

Jini Kilgore Ross, Editor

Judson Press ® Valley Forge

What Makes You So Strong? Sermons of Joy and Strength from
Jeremiah A. Wright, Jr.

© 1993
Judson Press, Valley Forge, PA 19482-0851

Bible quotations in this volume are from New Revised Standard Version of
the Bible, copyrighted 1989 by the Division of Christian Education of the
National Council of the Churches of Christ in the United States of America,
and are used by permission. All rights reserved. The Revised Standard
Version of the Bible, copyrighted 1946, 1952, 1971, 1973, by the division of
Christian Education of the National Council of the Churches of Christ in the
U.S.A., and used by permission. All rights reserved. (RSV); *The Holy Bible*,
King James Version (KJV); and the *Good News Bible*, the Bible in Today's
English Version. Copyright American Bible Society, 1976. Used by
permission (GNB).

Library of Congress Cataloging-in-Publication Data

Wright, Jeremiah A., Jr.
    What makes you so strong? : sermons of joy and strength from
Jeremiah A. Wright, Jr. / edited by Jini Kilgore Ross.
        p. cm.
    Includes bibliographical references and index.
    ISBN 0-8170-1198-6
    1. Sermons, American—Afro-American authors. 2. King, Martin
Luther, Jr., 1929-1968—Sermons. I. Ross, Jini Kilgore, 1948-
II. Title.
    BV4253.W75   1993
    252'.061—dc20   93-32716

Printed in the U.S.A.   94 95 96 97 98 99 00 01 02   10 9 8 7 6 5 4 3

Contents

Foreword

This book is a gem.

That sentence may at first read like an easily mouthed platitude. We give to many things, experiences, and people designations like "gem" or "jewel" or "precious," and so the very term dissolves into the commonplace. But a book of ten sermons by Dr. Jeremiah Wright lifts the label "gem" out of the realm of platitudes and vacuous compliments into dimensions of hard definition. It really is a gem.

The sermons in this book were delivered in two sets of an annual series of services commemorating the life, work, and theology of Dr. Martin Luther King, Jr. They were intended to reflect King's real role in history: not as civic or civil-rights activist, but as prophet-preacher, as pastor to the modern world, as spokesman for God to a fractured society. They were preached at Wheeler Avenue Baptist Church during the months of January 1990 and January 1991. Rev. Jini Kilgore Ross has done a remarkable job of keeping the flaming vitality in oral deliveries reduced to the printed page – no easy task. But when they are made available to a wider reading audience, they reveal not only the spirit of Dr. King, but the genius of one of the greatest preachers of this century.

And the book they constitute is a gem. The most casual glance at this book will convince even the hurried reader that he or she is in touch with one of the few collections of sermons that cannot easily be put down.

This book is extremely valuable. Whatever your question or hurt or need, it is touched in one or more of these incredible sermons, crafted by a man whose mastery of the language, whose breadth of understanding of human nature, whose incredible facility with ideas from the classics to rap, make him instantly conversant with scholars or children, with the deeply spiritual or novices to the faith.

This book is multifaceted. Through these pages walk the patriarchs of ancient Israel, the poets and prophets of the Exile, a barren woman and a favored queen, a capricious judge, and three devout young prisoners of war. These sermons display Wright's skill in eloquent profundity, in penetrating analysis, in whimsical levity that rivals the best stand-up comedy—and he exhibits all these in each message!

This book is the result of long years of much reading and the intense heat of inspiration by the Holy Spirit. Wright can devour the contents of a book a day, can tap into inner moods and feelings so that you would swear your best friend had gossiped about you to him, and can draw from the most raw human experiences indications of the presence, the power, and the mercy of God. That is not a capacity developed in college or seminary classrooms, nor a gift available to a naive adolescent. One must have read much, lived much, suffered much, and matured much to produce the shimmering beauty, the luminous iridescence, and the precise symmetry of these messages, through which the Light of the World sparkles in a multitude of hues and shades and tones.

This book is not just ten sermons. It is a wonder of insight, powerfully phrased truth, deeply probing discernment, and disarming closeups of saints and sinners. It is not even just good preaching. It is your soul and mine on paper. It is candid snapshots of God, brought to us in jeans, sneakers, and a baseball cap. It is a decahedral treasure.

It is a gem. And I am glad I was blessed to have Jerry Wright in my own lifetime.

William Lawson
Senior Pastor
Wheeler Avenue Baptist Church
Houston, Texas

Introduction

The sermons in this book come from the head and heart of a creative and imaginative preacher. Like a tour guide, Dr. Jeremiah Wright leads us on an excursion into the worlds of the Bible where we hear the sounds and smell the scents of the ancient world of queens and kings, peasants and poets, prophets and priests, saints and sinners. How strange it is that our tour guide helps us to see that we are at home in that world. The people we meet in the world of these biblical sermons are very much like ourselves, our families, friends, and foes. We return from the sermonic world of Dr. Wright cleansed and with clarity, conviction, and challenge. We are equipped for the living of these days and the facing of these hours.

A few creative preachers attract large audiences and are popular speakers for church conventions, college and university audiences, and seminary conclaves. Some of their sermons are sensational, even though they violate the laws of hermeneutical process. Good students of hermeneutics strive to correctly interpret a passage of Scripture. They seek the text in its original and earliest meanings and uses. Then they use the text as an aid in interpreting the present human situation. However, Jeremiah Wright takes us to a higher plateau of correct biblical exegesis and exposition that has both a universal application for all humankind and a special application to the particularity of the African American experience.

Dr. Wright's gifts and disciplined training in science, linguistics, history, philosophy, theology, and hermeneutics have placed him in the avant-garde of African American preaching. He marries the rationalism of the academy to the existentialism of the parish with wit and wisdom. Instead of simply interpreting the preaching passage from his academic and cultural richness, the spirituality of Dr. Wright crests like an ocean wave to a mysticism that allows God to address each hearer through the biblical text. This kind of preaching transforms lives.

No matter how well prepared a sermon is, the preacher must be prepared to present the sermon in an exciting, but acceptable manner. A well-written dull sermon puts hearers to sleep. The charm, charisma, and sincerity of Jeremiah Wright come through in these printed sermons. His humor is refreshing, yet Jeremiah Wright is no entertainer. After relaxing you with wit, he awakens your sleeping conscience with a prophetic jolt. Such preaching entertains, inspires, and greatly challenges the congregation to life transformation through continuing discipleship in Jesus Christ.

Dr. Jeremiah Wright has enriched my life with his preaching. The students whom I teach at the American Baptist Seminary of the West and the Graduate Theological Union are dismissed from their classes to hear him when he preaches at the Allen Temple Baptist Church of Oakland, California. The Allen Temple family, where I serve as senior pastor, use his sermon tapes for devotional and study purposes. One of my mentors, the late Dr. Jessie Jai McNeil, would call Dr. Wright a preacher prophet in mass society. Laypersons and clergy will find spiritual direction, practical wisdom, and life transformation in the pages of this book.

J. Alfred Smith, Sr., Senior Pastor
Allen Temple Baptist Church, Oakland, California and
Professor of Preaching and Christian Ministries,
American Baptist Seminary of the West, Berkeley, California

Unexpected Blessings

Mark 1:21-31

Have you ever been engaged in your normal routine when all of a sudden the Lord stepped in and blessed that situation beyond your wildest dreams? I like to call those instances the times of unexpected blessings.

The biblical record is replete with instances of unexpected blessings. In Genesis 21, Abraham and Sarah, who were way past the childbearing years (she was ninety, and he was one hundred), experienced one of God's unexpected blessings: a child. Sarah said, "God has brought me joy and laughter."

In Exodus 3, an African prince who was guilty of murder and was a fugitive from justice, lived in exile far away from the scene of the crime and way out of the jurisdiction of the court, with arrest warrants out on him and the statute of limitations passed in another time, in another country, in another life. With a new identity, Moses was happily married to a raven-black beauty and had several children. One day as he was tending his father-in-law's sheep on the back side of a mountain in Midian, he ran into one of God's unexpected blessings: a bush on fire and not on fire all at the same time. A voice unlike any other voice ever heard, coming from a God with a name as mysterious as the voice, was compelling him to lead his people – an unexpected blessing.

In 1 Samuel 1, a woman named Hannah prayed boldly for a child, but not just any child "as long as it's healthy." Instead, she was bold in her praying and told God she wanted a son. The prayer was answered, but far beyond her expectations. The boy she was given was to become the last of Israel's great judges. The boy who was born became the bridge between a judge named Samson and a king named Saul. The boy who was born (Samuel was his name) was the one called by God in Eli's house. Samuel was the one chosen by God to anoint and ordain the first two monarchs of the United Kingdom of Israel. Samuel was the one for whom all of Israel mourned for twenty-five years. Samuel was more than Hannah expected. He was an unexpected blessing.

The biblical record is replete with instances of unexpected blessings. Solomon prayed for wisdom, and God surprised him with unexpected blessings: more wealth, more treasure, and more fame than any king before him or after him. (See 2 Chronicles 1.)

A preacher named Isaiah, who was just doing his job up at the church house in the year that King Uzziah died, became the recipient of an unexpected blessing. You expect to be near God when you come into God's holy temple. You expect to feel God's presence when you cross over into holy precincts. That's because he promised that "where two or three are gathered in my name, I am there. . . ."[1] But Isaiah was blessed by the unexpected. He saw the Lord, high and lifted up, sitting on his throne with his train filling the temple. Isaiah saw the seraphim on fire with six wings—two covering his face, two covering his body, and two keeping it hovering in flight. He heard them hollering "Holy, holy, holy" back and forth with voices that shook the foundation, and he felt a hot burning coal taken from the altar and placed on his lips—cleansing, but not burning. Isaiah on an ordinary day up in the Lord's house was met in an extraordinary way and blessed with unexpected blessings beyond his wildest dreams.

The biblical record is replete with instances of unexpected blessings—folks following their normal routine, doing what it is they usually do, when all of a sudden the Lord steps in and blesses in ways that could not have been imagined. Therefore, it comes as no surprise that in the first chapter of Mark's Gospel there is one more instance of the Lord stopping by with unexpected blessings.

First, the passage says, "They went to Capernaum," the prophet Nahum's village, and the place where Jesus made his home away from home. He was originally, you'll remember, from Nazareth. But the folks in Nazareth were like the folks in our hometowns: they knew Jesus *when*. Because they knew Jesus *when*, they would not let him be what God wanted him to be. Not in their town. So he moved to Capernaum. His roots were in Nazareth, but he made his home in Capernaum. We find him in this passage on the Lord's day in the Lord's house. And I like that. Jesus went to church. A man – all man – in church.

Jesus Demonstrates the Importance of Worshiping at Church

Jesus went to church to worship God. In verse 35 of this chapter he is out all by himself, alone and praying. But this passage begins with him in the church. In fact, verse 39 says that wherever he went, whatever town he was in, the Lord's day found him in the Lord's house.

And when you read all of the biographies of Martin Luther King, that's one thing they omit. They talk about his training in Boston, his training at Crozier, his training at Morehouse. But King was a preacher. He went to church.

If Jesus went to church, don't you know a whole lot of people are on their way to hell believing that "you don't have to go to church." That's only half right. Let me give you the other half. You can worship God away from the church. You can worship God wherever you are. But you don't do one to the exclusion of the other. It is not either/or; it is both/and. You worship God both in the church and when you are away from the church. You don't stay away from the church and call yourself a follower of him who, wherever he was, went to church. No. It doesn't work like that. If Jesus went to church, who, in the name of all that is holy, do you think you are? Are you better than Jesus?

So we find Jesus in Capernaum, in the Lord's house, on

the Lord's day—Jesus in church. And then look at what happened. A man with an evil spirit came into the church.

The Devil Comes to Church, Too

The devil comes to church, too. I tell the folks at my church all the time, "The devil ain't got no other way of getting to church except we bring him." He came with this man in verse 23. Don't you know the devil will ride in your BMW, ride in your Mercedes Benz, get on public transportation right along with you, and when you get inside of the church, he'll break out all over the congregation. And you'll be wondering, "How did the devil get in the church?" He came with y'all. That's how.

Dr. Martin Marty, one of my mentors at the University of Chicago, told of a young white pastor and one of his old black female parishioners (the pastor pastored in a black community). On some Sundays this old woman would say, "Reverend, you sure did *teach* today. Umph, umph, umph!" Then on other Sundays she'd say, "You sure did *preach* today. Umph, umph!" One day this young pastor asked her, "Sister, what do you mean when you say I *teach*, and how is that different from when you say I *preach*?" The old woman said, "Well, Pastor, when you teach, God has given you something that you give me, and I can use it for that day and later on in the week, and get through the week—when you *teach*." She said, "When you *preach*, I can just feel God's presence, and he's hugging you real tight and he's pleased. You don't necessarily give me nothin' I can use, but I can feel God hugging you, and through you I can feel God hugging me. That's when you *preach*."

Then Marty said one Sunday when this pastor was severely upset by some political situation, he came and vented his spleen in what he thought was an excellently articulated exposition of God's will for that particular existential moment. At the door, this old woman said, "Reverend, I could feel God hugging you real close today, but I don't think he was pleased. In fact, it felt like he was crying while he was holding you tight." That's another way of saying the devil does come to church, sometimes with the parishioners and sometimes with the preacher. However the devil comes, he does come.

You see, the church is the primary recruiting station for the devil (a lot of church folks don't understand this). The devil does not need to go to a cocaine party. He's got those folks. He doesn't have to go there! Here's where folks are in danger of slipping away, so the devil comes to church and gets real busy.

"Just then," the Scripture says, "while Jesus was teaching," giving folks something to hold onto, something they could use in their lives, something to make a difference in the way they approached each day . . . while he was teaching like no one else ever taught (even the officers sent to arrest him said, "No man ever spoke like this man!"[2]), just then (verse 23) a man with an evil spirit came into the church.

Oh, the devil comes to church, all right, but he is no match for Jesus. Jesus can whip the devil every time. When Jesus gets in you, and you get in Jesus, in the Spirit, on the Lord's day, what does the Bible say? "Resist the devil and he will flee from you."[3] When you get in the Spirit and the Spirit gets in you, the devil acts like he's seen a ghost. And he has. He's seen the Holy Ghost. The devil is no match for the Spirit of Christ Jesus. The church folks say this man has authority to give orders to evil spirits and they obey him. The devil may come to church, but he's no match for the one who is Lord of the church, the one who said, "Upon this rock I will build my church; and the gates of hell shall not prevail against it."[4]

Taking Jesus Home

Immediately after church Jesus, his disciples, including James and John, left the church and went straight to Peter's and Andrew's house. Can you imagine taking Jesus home with you after church? There's some good news here in this passage for the married folks and the single folks. A lot of us like that part about being in the Spirit on the Lord's day, in the Lord's house, but at benediction time, too often for us, it's, "Later on, Jesus. Catch you next Sunday." This

passage suggests something new for some of us to try: taking Jesus home after church. Are you married like Peter?
Take Jesus home to where you live—up close with somebody
who knows all your warts and flaws and to where being a
Christian ain't all that easy. Or are you single like Andrew?
Take Jesus home to see those private places that we keep so
well hidden from the probing public. Can you imagine what
it would be like to take Jesus home with you tonight? Would
you have to straighten up the place? Or would you have to
straighten up your life?

Imagine Jesus sitting at the table with you, watching
you serve roasted preacher and warmed-over gossip. Imagine Jesus browsing through your books and your maga-
zines, even the ones that you keep hidden. Imagine Jesus
turning on your VCR to see what it is you watch when the
children are asleep. Jesus standing in the kitchen, listening
to you talking on the phone; Jesus hearing all you say and
seeing all you do. Not up here, where you've got all your holy
hats on, shouting "Praise the Lord," but at home, when your
hair is down and your shoes are off, and the real you is just
hanging all out.

Peter and Andrew took the Lord home, and what they experienced was an unexpected blessing. Peter had a wife.
After all, you can't have a mother-in-law unless you have a
wife. And here is Jesus all up in the midst of Peter's marriage. I've often thought that one of the reasons Peter wept
so bitterly, as it is recorded in the denial scenes, [5] was perhaps because of his memories about Jesus' impact on his
marriage and family life. It may be that Peter remembered a
loving relationship with his wife who, like a good friend, understood his compelling imperative to leave home for a
period of time and follow Jesus; he may have had that kind
of love in his marriage.

Memories will bring tears to your eyes—memories of the
kind of love that can only come when two people who are in
love and, who because of that love, make a home together
and grow from what each gives to the other. Those kinds of
memories will bring tears to your eyes—memories of a love
so deep that one of the African tribes has no word for it.

They call this type of love a "hurting in the heart." This hurt in the heart is so profound that just talking to the person on the phone starts you smiling, grinning, and acting silly. And ain't nobody in the room but you. Memories will bring tears to your eyes — memories of a shared moment of silence, perhaps in an embrace when nobody says a word, and just a hot tear of joy from cheek to chest says it all; memories of how life has taught you that love does not consist of gazing at each other, but in looking outward together in the same direction.

To have a reservoir of memories to fall back on when disaster hits is to be fortified against defeatism and despair. And to have Jesus as an integral part of your marriage, in your home, in your prayer life, in your private life, in your plan making and your lovemaking . . . Lord have mercy! No wonder Peter broke down.

Peter had a good thing, and the Lord was the center of his life and ministry. He took the Lord home and experienced an unexpected blessing.

It is not recorded anywhere that Andrew had a wife. But neither is it recorded anywhere that Andrew was defective or disadvantaged. First, he was the one who brought Peter to the Lord; and second, Jesus in this passage is in his home just as much as he is in Peter's home. Peter and Andrew, married and single, took the Lord home, and what they experienced was an unexpected blessing.

When they got home, Scripture says, Peter's mother-in-law was sick. No doubt she had been sick that morning when the others left for church. But they went to church anyhow. They had seen the Lord work in a marvelous way up at the church house, as the Lord will do every now and then. But then after church, they were going home and, if anything, the home situation had gotten worse. And isn't that how it is with us? Sometimes we leave home on Sundays, and things are in a turmoil. We meet the Lord at the Lord's house, and the Lord works in a mighty way in our souls, and we feel good; we feel great. Sometimes it feels like we've seen the seraphim that Isaiah saw. When we leave church, we can just feel the Lord hugging us and holding us, but when we get back home, things are no longer in a turmoil. They're in an uproar. Sometimes we hate to go home, because we know what's waiting for us there. But when you take Jesus home with you expect the unexpected.

The Lord Can Do Anything, Anywhere

When the churchgoers got home, Peter's mother-in-law was in bed with a fever. Somebody told Jesus about the situation. James Rowe composed a hymn about telling Jesus your problems. He wrote:

> Just tell Jesus, tell him all.
> Trials great and trials small.
> He will share them, freely bear them.
> Just tell Jesus, tell him all.

Elisha Hoffman put it another way in his hymn:

> I must tell Jesus all of my trials,
> I cannot bear these burdens alone;
> In my distress He kindly will help me,
> He ever loves and cares for His own.

When they took Jesus home and somebody told him about the situation, he went straight to Peter's mother-in-law, touched her, took her by the hand, and helped her up. One touch and the fever was gone.

Now this passage says at least two things that I want to impress upon you. First, it says the Lord works in your own house just like he works in the church house. If you meet the Lord here (in church) and take him there, he is as anxious to be with you there as he is to meet you here, and he will bless you unexpectedly.

The second thing this passage says is that Jesus is good for whatever ails you. The Bible does not say what the ailment was that had Peter's mother-in-law down. It doesn't say what the condition was that gave her a fever, and I'm glad it doesn't because in not saying, what it *is* saying is that Jesus can relieve any kind of suffering.

If you're sick, Jesus can make you well. Even if you're dying, Jesus can make up your dying bed. If you're depressed, Jesus can get you up. If you're down, Jesus can pick you up. If you've fallen, Jesus can hold you up. If you're in sin, Jesus can fix you up. Tempted and tried? Jesus can give you the victory. Where you're weak and defeated, his grace is still sufficient. Stained from sin? His blood can still wash you. In need of a savior? He still saves from the guttermost to the uttermost. He is good for whatever ails you. It does not make any difference what your situation is. If Jesus touches you, he'll bless you in really unexpected ways. He'll get you up from wherever you are and fix you up in ways you never imagined.

Praise Yields Unexpected Blessings

But the key to God's using and giving unexpected blessings is lost when we let problems get in the way of praise. Think about how problems in your life cause you to say, "I don't want to pray. Lord, just leave me alone." But when you praise God in spite of problems, it is precious, and it is priceless, and God will bless you unexpectedly. Peter and Andrew went to church anyhow and praised the Lord, and the Lord blessed them. They had a problem at home, but they went to the church to praise.

Dr. Charles Walker [6] tells a story that illustrates this for me. He was holding a revival in New England and the man who was assigned to take him back and forth every night to the hotel was a man who could not speak the king's English. He spoke good African American English, but he couldn't speak the king's English. He never did say "revival" the whole week. He said "vavibal." He said, "Rev., that 'vavibal' blessed me." The last night, as they headed to the airport Charles remarked that though the man didn't speak the king's English, he had "money's mammy." He was driving a Lincoln that was so high that Charles said he couldn't even read those roman numerals. He wore a three-carat diamond pinky ring, Brooks Brothers shoes, and a three-hundred-dollar suit. The man said, "Rev., you don't understand how I got this. I got it by putting the Lord first in my life and praising God in spite of problems."

Charles looked at him and the man continued, "See, folks see a car, they want to go get a car. They see a suit and a house, they try to get that. You know the Word says, Rev., 'Seek ye first the kingdom of God and his righteousness, and all these here things will be added unto you.' " The man said, "Let me tell you how I know that's true. Me and my wife been married over forty years. And during the depression I lost my job and we spent all of our life savings." And he said, "One Saturday night (both of us wanted to go to church the next morning and our church were eight miles away from where we lived, the bus fare were ten cents, and we only had fifteen cents to our names), my wife said, 'Honey, tell you what you do. What you do is you walk to church in the morning, and when you get to church you put a nickel in, and when you leave, you'll have a dime to ride back, 'cause it only cost a dime to ride in those days.

"And I got up, and I walked to church. I were tired, but it were a beautiful day, and as I were walking, I just felt blessed because I thought about people who didn't have no legs to walk. When I got to church, as soon as I stepped inside the sanctuary, the Holy Ghost said, 'Put the whole fifteen cents in.' And I started arguing with the Lord. I said, 'No, no. No, no. "Seek ye first" don't mean that. I done walked all the way here.' "

The man continued, "The choir started singing the processional. They were singing, 'How I got over. My soul looks back and wonders. . . .' But all I could hear them singing was, 'Put the whole fifteen cents in.' I stood there arguing with him. We read the responsive Scripture and the Word said, 'O give thanks unto the Lord for he is good.' But all I could see on that page was, 'Put the whole fifteen cents in.' When it came time for the offering, I lost the argument. I was rubbing my dime and my nickel together, and like a drum beating in my head, it kept beating over and over again, 'Put the whole fifteen cents in.' I put it in; I watched that offering plate take our last money in the world further and further away from me.

"But don't you know the Lord blessed me through the Word. The sermon that Sunday were, 'They that wait upon the LORD shall renew their strength. They shall mount up with wings as eagles.'⁷ When I left church I felt like one of them eagles. I was feeling good. I were ready to walk that eight miles back home.

"I got one block from the church and a strange lady stopped me. She said, 'Mister, I don't know you, and I don't know if you need work or not, but, here, take this address, and if you do need work they're hiring there tomorrow.' And I said, 'Thank you, Jesus.' I walked another block, and the Spirit of the Lord said, 'Look down.' When I looked down I seen a dime, and I said, 'Thank you, Jesus.' "

He concluded his story: "As soon as I picked the dime up, a bus were coming, and I said, 'Thank you, Jesus.' I got up on the bus, I put my dime in, and the bus driver give me back fifteen cents change. I said, 'Mister, I ain't give you no quarter; I give you a dime.' The bus driver said, 'Shut up, man, and sit down.' I said, 'Thank you, Jesus.'

"I got back home on the Lord's day, blessed by the Lord's Word, blessed by the Lord's work, blessed by the Lord with a job, blessed by the Lord with the same fifteen cents I left home with. And that job I went to the next day to interview, boy, I held that job for thirty-three years. Thank you, Jesus."

God will fix it for you. Won't he fix it? He's a good God!

I thank you, Jesus,
I thank you, Jesus,
I thank you, Lord.
Oh, you brought me from a mighty long way
A mighty long way.

I thank you, Jesus.
I thank you, Jesus.
I thank you, Jesus, I thank you Lord.
You brought me from a mighty,
A mighty long way.⁸

Study Questions

1. Choose one of the Old Testament accounts mentioned in the beginning of this sermon, and explain the unexpected blessing or blessings in the story.

2. Why is it important to worship with other believers in church? Of what significance is it to modern Christians that Jesus went to church to worship?

3. In what ways may we be guilty of ushering the devil into church? How is he no match for Jesus?

4. Reread the example of the elderly church sister who commented upon her pastor's teaching and preaching sermons. Why are both "head and heart" (knowledge and feeling) desirable attributes of a sermon?

5. Why is it especially important to continue praising and worshiping God when we have trying circumstances in our lives?

6. Just as Peter's mother-in-law received an unexpected blessing, we, too, may be so blessed. Recall the unexpected blessings in your life. Share your testimony with someone.

7. When Peter denied Jesus, he denied the personification of love. In what ways do we deny the love of Jesus by which he has directly and through others touched our lives?

8. Think of the man who, prompted by the Holy Spirit, gave all of his money in the offering. God blessed him materially. What unexpected spiritual blessings did you notice as he told his story?

9. Has this sermon given you a new insight or perspective? In what ways has it been encouraging or correcting?

Ain't Nobody Right but Us

Mark 9:33-41

Jesus said, "Whoever welcomes in my name one of these children, welcomes me . . ." (Mark 9:37, GNB). And when John heard the phrase "in my name," it triggered in his mind a problem that he and the others had confronted and that is still a problem in the church of Jesus Christ two thousand years later. Verses 33-37 introduce the issue of ego: I, me, and mine—looking out for number one. Which one of us is the greatest? the baddest? the toughest? the most together? the most spiritual? But right on the heels of the ego issue there surfaces what I call the flip side of the coin and that is this whole notion of the "in crowd," "our group," or what I call the "our gang" mentality. If you're not a part of our gang, then you're not a part of anything, cause "ain't nobody right but us."

Dr. James Forbes[1] calls this kind of thinking the "circling of the wagons mind-set"—us against the rest of the world. And you can see that kind of circling of the wagons mind-set clearly when you look at the Dutch Afrikaaner Church and the white racism that is so open and blatant in the doctrines of apartheid or in Zionism. That's *ain't nobody right but us* kind of thinking.

We can see the "our gang" mentality clearly when there is racism involved, but there are other places where this same kind of thinking rears its ugly head. When, for instance, Catholicism teaches that Protestants and Catholics can work together, worship together, pray together, walk together, do

everything together except take Holy Communion; when it
teaches that Catholics can share only among themselves the
body and blood of Jesus Christ, then what Catholicism in
effect is saying is "ain't nobody right but us." When Jehovah's Witnesses walk up and down the streets selling
Watchtower and *Awake!*, or when they come up on your
porch and stick their foot inside your door so they can share
with you, what Jehovah's Witnesses are saying is "ain't nobody right but us." When they can't attend a loved one's fu-
neral in a church other than their own, they are saying "ain't
nobody right but us." The thinking is, "If you're not doing it
our way, then you're doing it the wrong way." When the body
of Christ goes around saying that another part of the body
of Christ is wrong, "our gang" mentality is making itself
manifest.

Sometimes (and this is my tradition; I was born and
raised in it) the Baptists teach that everybody else's way of
baptizing is wrong. If you want to join their church, you've
got to be baptized all over again. The way you were baptized
in the Catholic, Episcopal, Lutheran, Methodist, Presbyterian, United Church of Christ, or Pentecostal tradition is
wrong. It's like a vaccination that didn't take. What they
are saying is "It doesn't belong to our group. It doesn't fit in
with what we teach."

Sometimes it's the Pentecostals who teach that same
song in a different key. They say, "What words were used at
your baptism?"

"Oh, I was baptized in the name of the Father, the Son,
and the Holy Ghost."

"Umph umm. Them are the wrong words, honey. Those
words don't belong to our group. They don't fit in with what
we teach. You gotta be baptized all over again in the name
of Jesus, hallelujah!" Outside of the blatant racism that allows us to see clearly what this "our gang" mentality is doing are countless other places where this same *ain't nobody
right but us* kind of thinking shows up, and keeps on showing up.

The problem that John and the others confronted is still
a problem within the church two thousand years after that
confession in Capernaum. When Jesus said "in my name,"

John said, "Teacher, we saw a man who was driving out demons in your name" (Mark 9:38, GNB). Think about that for
a moment. Was the man blaspheming? No. Was he taking
the Lord's name in vain? No. Was he talking bad about the
master? No. Was he being disrespectful. No. Was he making
fun of the fairest of ten thousand? No. What was he doing?
He was doing what the disciples themselves could not do
(see verse 18). This man was demonstrating, according to
verse 29, what a powerful prayer life he had, showing by
deed what a powerful hook-up to divinity he had. He believed in prayer. He believed in Jesus. Jesus had said that
only prayer could drive this kind of demon out. And here
was this man, obviously a praying man, driving out demons
in the name of Jesus. Was he hurting people? No. Was he
teaching some heretical doctrine? No. It was in the name of
Jesus, healing; in the name of Jesus, wholeness; in the name
of Jesus, a brand new you. In the name of Jesus.

Well what was the problem? The disciples told him to
stop because "he's not one of our gang. He doesn't belong to
our group." This problem of who is the greatest is closely
related to another problem of *us* versus *them*: "Ours is the
only way to a right relationship with the Lord. Our way is
the only way to salvation. Our group is the one to which you
must belong if you want to be right. And our definition of
discipleship is the only definition that is operable and acceptable."

Please note: this is not an argument against demonic
forces outside the church trying to attack the church or destroy it. No. This is an argument, first of all, about degrees
of greatness among disciples. And then there is a second argument among disciples about being different.

Here was a man who believed in prayer. Here was a man
who believed in Jesus. Here was a man who believed in the
power of Jesus' name. Here was a disciple of Jesus, who has
all power, doing what the other disciples could not do. The
only problem was that he was different. He did not belong
to the right group.

Do you have any idea what that feels like? Do you have
any idea how much we still perpetuate this problem, confessed by John in Capernaum? I'm not talking only about

denominational differences, but about differences among
disciples within the same denomination. Those disciples
who tend to be intellectual put down disciples who tend to
be emotional. This past year after an eleven o'clock service
on Sunday I drove up from Chicago to Grand Rapids. The
Deltas sorority had asked me to preach at their annual service focusing on African American youth. They thought I
had a message that young people needed to hear. Well, these
Deltas had never heard of the United Church of Christ, so
they looked in the phone book under "United Church of
Christ," and they found there were sixteen such congregations there in Grand Rapids. They invited them all to come
hear Jeremiah Wright, not knowing that our denomination
has 6,500 congregations, 288 of them black. So all of these
white folks showed up to hear me talk to African American
youth. But the Deltas had invited me to preach, and I
preached.

After the service was over, one of the white men there, a
member of our denomination, came up to me grinning. He
was so proud. He was proud to be a member of our denomination and proud that I was a member of the same denomination. He said to me, "Man, you combine the best of both
worlds. You've got the intellectual content from the white
world and the emotional content from the black world."
Then he realized that didn't sound too good, so he tried to
fix it up. He said, "Ha, ha, ha, ha. We need more preachers
just like you." Still not satisfied, he kept on going, "You
know, our white preachers tend to not express what they
feel in the same manner."

Whenever we encounter disciples who are different, we
tend to put them down. We tend to say in so many subtle
ways that "if you ain't like us, then you ain't right, 'cause
ain't nobody right but us." And I have discovered that these
put-downs, whether by John and his partners in Capernaum
or by us and our colleagues in today's church, stem from at
least three sources.

First, there is the misconception that being different
means being deficient. Second, the put-down of the disciples
who are different comes from our own insecurities and un-

certainties about who we are. And third, we put down disciples who are different because of what we see, or to be more
precise, because of the vast difference between what we see
and what God sees.

Being Different Does Not Mean Being Deficient

We tend to classify folks who are not like us as somehow
being substandard, below the norm, not quite up to par.
They are deficient. In the field of education, the entire Eurocentric educational system was based on the fallacious assumption that every normal person was a left-brain person
when it came to cognition and learning styles. Think about
the whole Eurocentric educational system. Children in cribs
are provided with mobiles of certain shapes. This is a circle.
This is a cube. This is a triangle. That's how they learn their
colors and their shapes. Leave them with an object because
left-brain people are object-oriented: they relate to objects.
Later on you can leave them with a book, and they will learn
from the book.

On the other hand, right-brain people, such as Africans
and African Americans, are not object-oriented; they are
people-oriented. When integration first came, back in the
fifties, and whites had black kids in their classrooms for the
first time, the white teachers did not know what to do, because the black kids kept getting in their space. The children wanted to touch them and hang on them and talk to
them, because that's how black children are. In Africa
mothers carry their children for two or three years. They're
used to contact. They breast-feed for longer periods of time.
They don't care what the book says because they're people-
oriented, not object-oriented. It took educators like Janice
Hale Benson[2] to come along and point out that African children (and Jesus was African) have different ways of learning, different cognition styles, because they are
right-brained. That doesn't mean they are deficient; it simply means that they are different. Difference is not synonymous with deficiency.

In the field of speech, linguistics, and lexicography (up
until twenty or twenty-five years ago), the assumption was

that African American dialect was deficient. Everybody else in America had a dialect (a pattern of speaking that differs in sound, grammar, and vocabulary), but African Americans were told, "You speak bad English." The truth of the matter is that we all speak different dialects of English. If you don't believe me, just ask the British. They'll tell you as soon as you open your mouth, "Oh, you're from America," because they recognize your accent and know you're not speaking the king's English.

The truth is that every ethnic and geographic group in this country speaks a different dialect. Remember John F. Kennedy back in 1960, standing out in front of the Capitol being inaugurated as president saying, "Eeask not what your country can do for you. Eeask, rather, what you can do for your country."

That's not good English. That's a New England, Boston-American dialect. It's very different from Lyndon Baines Johnson from Texas, who said, "My fellow Uhmarikans."

Some midwesterners put two syllables on the letter *a*. For *my dad* they say *my dee-ad*. I never will forget that the first day after I had moved to Chicago I went out shopping to buy a few things trying to fix up the house, and the saleslady said, "You want this in a *beeag*?" I said, "In a big what?" She said, "In a *beeag*?" I said, "Oh, yeah, put it in a *beeag*." That's very different from the West African *a* which has no diphthong.[3] It's an *ah* sound. Which is deficient: John F. Kennedy's *eeask*, Lyndon Johnson's *Uhmarikans*, or the Midwesterner's *beeag*? African American children say *a* like *rat now*, *rat cheer* (for right now and right here).

In Washington, D.C., in the late sixties, I worked in a federally funded program to teach English as a second language to African Americans. In fact, you can pick up Geneva Smitherman's[4] book today and see in print things we were teaching twenty-five years ago. Linguistic researchers found out that African Americans had a dialect and that people needed to learn how to communicate with us. Educators had to stop saying, "You speak bad English," and instead say, "You have a perfectly legitimate dialect." Of course, African Americans still had to remember that there is another dialect used in corporate America, at the phone company, and at the gas company. If you want a job with them, you don't go in there saying, "Yo, what is? What up?" You have to learn this other language.

When linguists and speech pathologists did an interdisciplinary study and looked at the languages of West Africa, out of which slaves had been brought into this country, they began to find some fascinating facts. They found that in those languages there were no fricatives, as there are in the Indo-European, Germanic languages. There are no hard endings; none of their words end *like* this. They're all open at the end: Kwame Nkrumu, Nigeria, Liberia, Ghana, Accra, Abidjan. All open and soft. English doesn't have word endings like that.

Then they found out there are no tenses in the verbs of African languages. Just like many other Semitic languages, you can tell the tense of a verb by the context of the sentence in which it is used. For instance, the verb to express movement from one place to the other place is "go." "What did you do yesterday?" "Me *go* work." "What you do this evening?" "Me *go* church." "What you do tomorrow?" "Me *go* back work." *Go.* Always *go.* Not I *went*, I *will have gone*, I *shall go*. No, it's *go*. And I said "me" on purpose, because the pronouns do not decline. It's always *me*. It's not *I, my, mine.* No, it's *me*."

Then they discovered that the verb "to be" has a whole special use in West African language. You omit the verb "to be" when you want to talk about immediacy. You insert the verb "to be" when you want to show an ongoing activity. For example, "Where your mama?" means "Where is she rat now?" What's the answer? "She at home." Not, "Where *is* your mother?" "She *is* at home." You leave *is* out. If you want to show ongoing activity, you say, "What your mama do on Sunday?" "She *be* going to church." You stick *be* in there to show continuity.

They also found out that there are no consonant clusters in any of the West African languages. You don't have *st*: "I was *just* playing" becomes "I *jes* playing." How many times have black people been ridiculed when they said, "I want to *axk* you a question"? There is no *sk* sound in West African languages.

There also aren't any *th* sounds. You don't have *this* and *that*; it's *dem*. Sometimes at the beginning of a word it's *dis* and *dat*, and at the end of a word it's an *f* such as, "I'm gonna punch you in your *mouf*." And for those of you who are from the "ghetto" it's a *v* in the middle of a word, *muhvah, your muhvah*. No *th* sound. No *st* sound. No consonant clusters. No diphthongs.

We laugh at the Pennsylvania Dutch who say, "Throw papa from the train, his hat" because the direct object comes at the end of the sentence, but what happens is that they took the English vocabulary and stuck it in their Dutch word order. *Papa gone now!*

But there's another aspect to learning language: how do people under oppression learn a foreign language? Inevitably, people under oppression learn a code language in order to talk to each other right in front of "the man" without him having the slightest idea about what they're saying.[5] And that still goes on in some of the places where oppressed people work every day. Listen to the folk at lunchtime: "What it be like?" "Ain't nothin' to it." "What's up?" What are they talking about? And as soon as outsiders pick up on one word, the code changes and is made into something else. This is "good morning": "What's up?" "Straight up." "Understan' what I'm sayin'?" Not, "Do you understand what I'm saying?"

Then there is the problem of group reinforcement, which means that your native group will make you speak a certain way. Dr. Stanley Alsop, who taught me most of what I know about linguistics, earned a Ph.D. in linguistics from Oxford. He was dean of the Jamaican campus of the University of the West Indies. He spent twenty years collecting Africanisms in the English language. He said that he could study all of this at Oxford and do a Ph.D. at Oxford, "but when I go home to Montego Bay, mahn, I got to go home talking like the people from Jamaica, otherwise they want to know, 'What's the matter? You come back wif yo mouf all full de white man language?' "

And the same is true in African America. I spent six years at the University of Chicago Divinity School in a Ph.D. program, a nice clustered island of whiteness on the south side of Chicago, and we could be very erudite over there—very, very intellectual. But once you come out of the white environment and cross into the black community, you don't come out saying, "What is happening, my man?" No, no. The group will make you talk like they talk. Then, in addition to group reinforcement, don't forget early childhood. When are children's speech patterns fixed for life? By the time they're four years old.

Look at the field of dance. There was a white man named Arthur Murray who made millions of dollars by putting in a book how you learn to dance. He put black feet for the heavy beats and white feet for the off beats. The man made a million dollars. But see, for right-brain people, you cannot put in a book how to dance. How are you going to put M.C. Hammer[6] in a book? That won't go in your book. You can't touch that.[7]

Listen to music playing. White people tend to clap on the beat; black people tend to clap off the beat. It's just different, that's all; not that one is deficient. Different is not synonymous with deficient. Yet, when we encounter different disciples, we often classify them as deficient. We put them down—intellectual, emotional, heterosexual, denominational. It doesn't matter. If you don't belong to our group, there's something wrong, cause "ain't nobody right but us." I have been teaching this truth in my seminary classes and music classes for years, and still it is a difficult truth to hear, to accept, and, even more difficult to live. Difference is not synonymous with deficiency.

Our Identity: Insecurities and Uncertainties

The second source of put-downs of disciples who are different comes from our own insecurities and uncertainties about who we are. We try to build ourselves up by putting other folk down. We do it in elementary school, and some of us are still doing it with two or three degrees from graduate school. We put other folk down in an attempt to build up our own self-worth. We're insecure and uncertain as to who we are.

John and his partners were insecure because they could not do what this other disciple could do. So they put him down in an attempt to build up their sagging estimates of their own self-worth. They might not have had his ability, but he didn't have access to their fraternity. He didn't belong to their group.

When you are secure about who you are and whose you are, you don't have to put other folk down in an attempt to build yourself up. Who you are is not determined by how small somebody else is made to look or how big you are made to look in comparison with somebody else. Who you are is determined by whose you are. And when you are the Lord's, then that becomes the primary relationship, not how you are viewed in relationship to somebody else who also belongs to the Lord. Jesus said, "Don't try to stop him. He's doing this in my name. Whoever is not against us is for us" (Mark 9:39-40, author's paraphrase).

You are secure when you belong to Jesus. You are secure enough to let other folk who also belong to Jesus be who they are as he made them. You don't have to make them over in your image or go behind God and redo what God has already done. You have the freedom to let other disciples have their space and do wondrous things in the name of Him who has already done great things for you.

When you try to build yourself up by tearing somebody else down, it shows you are weak; it shows you are insecure; it shows your ignorance; it shows your arrogance. It makes you just like others who have tried to build themselves up by degrading, downplaying, and disparaging everything that somebody else ever did. Historically, Europeans tried to build themselves up by tearing down all that Africans had done. But you can't make yourself something by saying somebody else is nothing.

You don't have to build yourself up by tearing somebody down. I don't have to do that. Don't you know I'm somebody because I'm Mary and Jeremiah Wright's boy? I'm somebody because Jesus gave his life for me. I'm somebody because Jesus hung on a cross for me. I'm somebody because Jesus loves and cares for me. I am somebody because Jesus said he was coming back for me.

What We See and What God Sees

The third thing I've discovered about the source of put-downs (the apostle Paul gives us a clue when he says we see through a glass darkly) is that we put down disciples who are different because of what we see or, to be more precise, because of the vast difference between what we see and what God sees. In Mark 9:38 John says, "We saw a man. . . ." And don't you know that we have that same tendency. We see. And the way we see things is not the way God sees them. We saw a man or we saw a denomination or we saw a church. We see compartmentally. All we can see is our own compartment, our own little categories.

One of the biggest problems in the church universal (Dr. King talked about it twenty-seven years ago) is seeing our little arc of the circle and equating that tiny little arc with the whole circle. You can't see the whole circle. Only God can see the whole circle. We see compartmentally, but God sees completely. We see like those blind men, each one feeling a different part of an elephant—one describing the trunk and the other the tusk and the leg. God sees the whole elephant. We see partially, but God sees the whole.

We see prejudicially: "He doesn't belong to our group." But God sees paternally, or parentally: "They all belong to me. Those are all my children." We see exclusively. We exclude certain people. We exclude certain types: "our gang" versus "them." We see exclusively, but God sees inclusively: All ye come unto me. God so loved the world that he gave his only begotten son that whosoever—everybody can come. We only see what we can see right now, our finitude; but God sees infinitely.

Then, we see competitively. We're always competing with one another. Those of you who have sisters or brothers might know something about competing with our sisters and brothers to win the favor of Mommy and Daddy.

Before my baby daughter was born, we knew she would

be a girl, and we had already named her. My stepson, who was experiencing some of that sibling competition, had marked off her bedroom with his feet. He said, "Mama, Jamila's bedroom is bigger than mine and Nicole's." And his mother very wisely handled this. She said, "Go speak to your father."

He came in to speak to me and I said, "Son, please don't think that we love one child more than we love the other child. First of all, that's not Jamila's room. That is the guest room. Her crib is in there right now. When she gets older, she'll be down the hall with you all. But, number two, look at your two older sisters, Janet and Jerry, and understand I love our children because of who they are."

We're always trying to compete. God does not look that way. God looks compassionately: "His compassions fail not. They are new every morning. . . ."[8]

We always want to go to God and talk to God in terms of what our needs are, and in this competitive mode we start seeing other preachers as our competitors. It may not happen in your city, but in Chicago you could tell folks, "Jesus is preaching at Trinity next week," and somebody would say, "Well see if you can't get him to come over here because I'm not going over there to hear him."

We're always trying to compete with each other. And, you know, members will set you up like that too. Members will say, "I like the way you preach better than that other preacher." But those aren't your competitors. When John and the disciples saw that man casting out demons, they thought he was competing with them. Jesus said that people like that aren't your competitors. Those are your companions.

You need every last one of those preachers. We need one another. We have enough crack cocaine in our community and enough ignorance in our community to be working from now until Jesus comes. Those aren't your competitors. Those are your companions. We need each one of the ministers of the gospel working together. We need our churches working together.

The next time you're tempted to say, "Ain't nobody right but us," remember that differences aren't necessarily synonymous with deficiencies. Remember that you can't build yourself up by tearing somebody else down. Remember that in the Lord we don't have competitors. We have companions.

Study Questions

1. Explain what is meant by this quote from the sermon: "We put down disciples who are different . . . because of the vast difference between what we see and what God sees."

2. Does avoiding *ain't nobody right but us* thinking when we converse with people who have different religions and doctrines weaken our own witness? If not, tell how one can strongly maintain one's own beliefs while avoiding *ain't nobody right but us* thinking.

3. Can you think of a time when being different in some way made you feel that you were personally deficient? Did you regard differences in others as deficiencies? What is offered as an antidote to this type of thinking about ourselves or others?

4. What unique language do all Americans have in common? Why is it that dialects have been acceptable in groups other than African Americans?

5. Jesus observes that the man is casting out demons in his name. Think about what it means to do something in Jesus' name.

6. Jesus' words "Whoever is not against us is for us" are thought-provoking. Our inclination is to say "but . . . ."

However, Jesus closes the conversation with this short and pointed statement. Apply it to some situation in your own life. Explore the concept of "against" in the statement.

7. It is easy to tear others down without realizing that we are trying to build up ourselves. Reflect on ways in which we commonly do this. Is there a hidden trace of insecurity, ignorance, weakness, or arrogance in our actions?

8. Someone has once wisely noted that we should not judge others because we do not know where they've been, where they are now, or where they're going. Apply this thought to the section on "What We See and What God Sees."

9. How can we eliminate competition among the fellowship of believers? How can we foster a better sense of being on the same team with one another?

10. We can't be close to everyone, so we naturally exclude people who are different or with whom we feel uncomfortable. Is this practice all right as long as we do not harbor prejudices toward others, or should we consciously try to associate with persons who are different from ourselves?

Unhitch the Trailer

Genesis 45:1-5; 50:15-26

Joseph, the grandson of Isaac, could have been a prime candidate for some long-term therapy with any one of the qualified psychiatrists practicing in North Africa around 1,500 years before the birth of Christ. Joseph had every right to have been one of the good-paying customers on a psychologist's couch somewhere in the posh section of Cairo, coming in once a week to get his head screwed back on straight after his own family had seen to it that it was screwed on crooked.

Joseph was disliked for something over which he had no control, disliked because of the way he had been born. Verse 3 of chapter 37 (GNB) says, "Jacob loved Joseph more than all his other sons, because he had been born to him when he was old." The way he was born caused him to be disliked by his jealous brothers. Who anywhere has any control over the way he or she was born? Do you know what it's like being disliked because of the way you were born?

We know something about what this is like. We who are black don't like it one bit when a white person dislikes us because we were born black. We don't like it one bit when Europeans set the standards of beauty by telling us that thin lips are pretty and full lips are ugly. When Europeans tell us that thin noses are pretty and broad noses are ugly, we don't like it.

But what about when it is we who dislike ourselves? Do you have any idea what it is like when your own kind doesn't like you because of the way you were born: black folk not liking yellow folk because they're yellow, red bones not liking dark ones because they're dark. It sounds like Miriam and Aaron in Numbers 12, doesn't it?[1]

Do you have any idea what that is like? Folk can't help what color they were born. God made them that way. They had no control over that, yet some of our own kind don't like others of our own kind because of what God did, because of the way we were born.

When I was growing up, folks used to buy a bleaching cream called Nadinola to try to change what God had done. Our dads wore stocking caps to make their hair lie down smoothly like somebody else's. Some of us still do this. We dislike what God gave us because somebody taught us that what we have is defective and substandard.

From the time I was in the second grade until my twenty-first birthday, I had a best friend. Our friendship started off in the weirdest way. Every day at three-fifteen, my friend would beat me up. I hated to see three-fifteen coming because I knew I'd get a whipping on the way home. I would try a different route, but he would always cut me off. He lived one block from me. No matter which way I'd try, he'd be there waiting for me. He was bigger than I was. What I did not know at the time was how much older he was. I knew he was in fourth grade—two grades ahead of me—but I didn't know he was five years older than I. He had been left back three times. I would go home and tell my mama that this boy in the fourth grade was beating me up, and she would try to make a man of me. She wanted me to stand up and fight back.

I said, "Mama, I'm trying to fight him back, but he's bigger than I am." She said, "Well, equalize the difference in your sizes." I said, "How is that?" She said, "When he hits you, fall on a stick. When you come up, that will close the gap in your sizes."

So the next day, I waited for three-fifteen. And when he hit me, I fell on a sewer cover and tried to pick it up. He broke out laughing at me. He said, "You can't pick that up. What you gonna do with it?"

Just like that we became friends. Just like that! We walked to and from school every day, and he came up to our church and joined our church. In about four or five months, after we got to be good buddies, I said, "Why did you fight me every day like that, beating me up?" He said, "My mama say we don't trust yellow people." He was very big and very dark.

I didn't know what he was talking about, so I went home and asked my parents. They said they thought they had left all of that foolishness down in Virginia with the house slave, field slave stuff. They told us all about the color problem within the African American community. They thought they'd never have to teach us that in Philadelphia, but they did. And the whole time we were friends, I was never allowed in his house. I could go on his porch, but I couldn't go in his house because of what his mama said. He came down to my house, and we hung out. We got to be thick as thieves; in fact, we'd pick fights. They used to call us "Vanilla Fudge." If there was somebody we didn't like, we'd walk up to him and say, "Now, which one of us is the darkest?" Whatever that brother said was wrong.

On my twenty-first birthday (and back in those days twenty-one meant you were grown, not eighteen), I was a Marine stationed at Camp Lejeune. My friend was stationed at Camp Cherry Point. In fact, I had gone into the Marine Corps because of him. Since I could not get leave from the base, he came down from his base and we hung out together the whole day. Camp Lejeune had ten thousand people stationed there, and that meant there were about forty-five bars on the base, and we tried to find every last one of them.

When we got back to my area that night, he said, "Buddy, I got something to tell you." And I said, "What's that, man?" He said, "You remember how we used to fight when we were little?" I said, "If you call hitting me and me hitting the ground a fight, yeah, I remember that." He said, "Do you remember why we used to fight?" I said, "I can't ever forget why we used to fight. Sure, I remember that. Your mama said you don't trust yellow people."

He said, "Well, I got something I can't live with no longer. I gotta tell you. I gotta get it off me today." And he went on to tell me that he had never gotten over what his mother told him. I said, "What are you talking about?" You know, this was my twenty-first birthday.

What he was talking about was that he had been pretending to be my friend all those years. And I said, "Why the pretense?" And he said he liked my sister, and he knew he could be in my house if he was pretending to be my friend. So all those years, the man I thought was my best friend was not a friend to me at all, and he did not like me because of the way I had been born. Like Joseph, I was disliked for something over which I had absolutely no control.

Dreams Are Given by God

Then, the gift God gave Joseph caused him to be disliked even more. God gave him the gift of dreams and dream interpretation. That was not something he picked up along the way. That was not some little trick Joseph learned down in the Casbah at Cairo.[2] Nobody goes to sleep at night saying, "Well, tonight I think I'm going to dream about such and such."

No, no. A dream is another thing over which you have no control. And biblical dreams especially were known throughout Bible days to be given by God. Jacob dreamed at a place called Beth-el, house of God.[3] He dreamed he saw a stairway, a ladder, going up and coming down with angels on it. He dreamed that the Lord stood beside him and said, "I am the LORD, the God of Abraham your father and the God of Isaac." And today, because of Jacob's dream, we still sing in our church "We are climbing Jacob's ladder." In biblical days dreams were known and understood to be given by God.

In Daniel 7, continuing all the way through Daniel 12, the prophet, the preacher, the man of God describes the terrible and powerful things that he saw in a dream. When Mary's fiancé, Joseph of Nazareth, found out that Mary was pregnant before they were married, Matthew 1:20 (GNB) says, "While he was thinking about this, an angel of the Lord appeared to him in a dream and said, '. . . you will name him Jesus. . . ." And today, because of that dream, we still call him Jesus.

When the sable sages from the East came with their gifts of gold, frankincense and myrrh, Herod tried to use them in his nefarious plot, but Matthew 2:12 says they returned to their country by another road because God had warned them in a dream not to go back to Herod.

The very next verse says that after the wise men had left, an angel of the Lord appeared in a dream to Joseph and told him to get up and take his wife and his child further south into Africa and stay there "until I tell you to leave." Then, Matthew 2:19 (GNB) says that after Herod died, an angel of the Lord appeared to Joseph in a dream in Africa and said, "Get up, take the child and his mother, and go back to the land of Israel, because those who tried to kill the child are dead."

In Matthew 27, when Jesus was about to be sentenced by Pontius Pilate, verse 19 (GNB) says while Pilate was sitting in the judgment hall, his wife sent him a message saying, "Have nothing to do with that innocent man, because in a dream last night I suffered much on account of him."

Then, in preparation for the Day of Pentecost and the years of preaching after the resurrection, Peter quoted the prophet Joel, who said, "And it shall come to pass afterward that I will pour out my spirit upon all flesh; and your sons and your daughters shall prophesy [proclaim and preach my message], your old men shall dream dreams, and your young men shall see visions.[4]

In biblical days, dreams were known and understood to be given by God. Joseph dreamed and interpreted dreams, and his own folk didn't like it because of what God gave him.

Joseph Was Disliked

First, Joseph was not liked because of the way he was born, the way God made him. Then he was not liked because of the gift he had, what God gave him. Next, he got in trouble because he did the right thing.

Genesis 39:6 says that Joseph, who was well-built and good-looking (a Billy Dee face on a Mike Tyson body), got next to Mrs. Potiphar. His boss's wife just couldn't stand being around that fine hunk, so she asked him to go to bed with her. Now, normally we tend to think of the man as the one who does the asking, and normally we expect that there will be some repercussions, especially if you hit on a married woman. But when you didn't do the hitting, and when all you did do was refuse to participate in something illegal and immoral, and you're the one that ends up behind the eight ball, and you're the one going to jail for doing something that was right, then you can see why I say Joseph would have been an excellent candidate for a therapist's couch.

He was disliked because of the way God made him. He was disliked because of the gift God gave him. And he was disenfranchised because he acted in a way God would have wanted him to act. And then he was disregarded by the very one to whom he was a blessing. Chapter 40, verse 23 says that the wine steward whose dream he interpreted while they both were in prison never gave Joseph another thought. He forgot all about him instead of recommending his release to the pharaoh as he had promised to do.

Disliked, disenfranchised, and disregarded! First, it was his step-brothers, then it was Pharaoh's wife, then it was the steward. Joseph was carrying around a lot of excess baggage with a lot of stored up grievances – undeserved wrongs done to him, unmerited mess dumped on him – things over which he had no control. Joseph had a long list of stuff that he could have deposited in the memory banks of his mind and allowed to ride and draw interest until the day that it was his turn to be in a position to do something about all those folk who had been doing wrong to him.

The Temptation to Get Even

Remember: "Every dog has his day" and "What goes around comes around." Many times we get caught in the quicksand of past mistakes, past failures, and things done to us like Joseph had done to him. We can't seem to let go of the problems or pain that we did not deserve. Every time we think about them, we get mad all over again. Every time we try to talk about them, we get hot or we get hurt all over, and sometimes we start crying out of anger and frustration all over again. Sometimes the thought of payback consumes us. You've seen those bumper stickers that say, "I don't get mad. I get even."

That's what Joseph's brothers were afraid of. Yes, he had welcomed them and cried with loud sobs at the reunion, and he had been very spiritual about his perspective, but when Daddy died (Genesis 50), the brothers got scared because they thought Joseph might think the same way they thought.

How would you feel if somebody had messed over you in the way they messed over him? Joseph's brothers said, "What if? What if Joseph still hates us and plans to pay us back for all the harm we did to him?"

What if you had the power that Joseph had? He was thirty-seven years old, the number two person in all the country with the pharaoh's authority and permission to do whatever he felt like doing. What if you could make Reagan experience what it's like to be poor with no education, no job, and no hope, plus no law you can count on to protect you and no court in which you can get a fair hearing? What if you could pay back all of those old mean white folks who are skinheads or in the Klan or riding around in police cars with guns, thinking that white is right and white is superior and all the coloreds belong back in slavery? What if you could pay them back?

What if you could get back at the folk who made your mama ride in the back of buses, use segregated and inferior facilities, and feel like she was less than a person because of her color? What if you could get your hands on those white folk in South Africa right now who refuse to see blacks as human beings? Yes, Nelson Mandela is free, but he still can't vote.

What if you could get in your power for one hour that rascal who put your family member on cocaine? What if you could pay back that person who hurt you so bad you can never forgive him? What if you could do whatever you

wanted to and not ever have to worry about trouble, repercussions, or reprisals—not go to jail, not do any time, not
have anybody question anything you did?

To that "ex" of yours or to that incestuous relative of
yours or to that person who changed your life forever for the
worse or to that supervisor of yours or to that person you
just can't stand—what if you could get him or her and not
have to worry about anybody saying anything? That's the
position Joseph was in. It is no wonder his brothers asked,
"What if?" What if Joseph still hates us and plans to pay us
back for all of the harm? Please notice that the Scripture
never said that Joseph ever hated them. But they knew
that's how they would have felt if someone had done to them
what they did to him. When they put themselves in Joseph's
position, they were afraid that Joseph would get even.

Breaking the Cycle of Pain with God's Perspective

But Joseph was in another place altogether. And the
place that Joseph was in shows us that there is a way of
breaking the cycle of pain, no matter how deep the pain is,
and no matter how permanent we think the pain might be.
How was King able to hold on to an ethic of nonviolence in
the midst of the most violent society in the world? How was
he able to get to a place of forgiveness when his life was
choked with the bitterness of Birmingham, the stench of
Selma, the meanness of Memphis and Montgomery? How
did he find the strength to love in the midst of a sea of hatred?

There is a way of breaking the cycle of pain and moving
forward with our lives. Somebody wants to know how. Well,
first we need to use God's perspective. God's perspective
helps us to see things in a different way, from a different
vantage point, and with a different angle of vision. God's
perspective helps us to keep a balanced view of our problems, our potential, and our possibilities.

Joseph had a good grasp of God's perspective. His brothers thought of him as an enemy. They treated him like the
enemy, despised him because of the way he had been born,
hated his guts, and could not stand him horseback riding or
walking. They talked about him behind his back, plotted

against him while he was unaware, sold him into slavery, never giving him a second thought, and lied on him and lied about him. He said to them, "I am your brother." That's God's perspective.

Then Joseph said, "Do not be upset or blame yourself because you sold me out, because it was really God who sent me ahead of you to save people's lives. God had a purpose that neither you nor I could understand then." That's God's perspective. And when they started to panic because of the possibility of payback, Joseph said to them, "Don't be afraid. I wouldn't try to play God in your life. I just thank God. You plotted evil against me, but God has turned it around into good."

This is God's perspective, a situation seen from God's angle. How did the apostle Paul put it? "All things work together for good for those who love God, who are called according to his purpose."[5] We know that in all things God is working. God's perspective helps us to see things in a different way. When we are down on ourselves and focusing solely on our failures, we need God's perspective to help get us up out of that ditch. While we are feeling that we are no good because we blew it, God, who loves us, is smiling and saying, "That's my child. My child made a mistake, but my child is more than that one mistake. Just watch what my child can do." God's perspective helps us keep our perspective not only on our problems but also on our potential and on our possibility.

I get a glimpse of what God's perspective is like every time I have to stand up and preach in front of my mother and father. When I go home to Philadelphia to preach, or to New Jersey, Baltimore, or Howard University, my daddy, who is eighty-one, and my mama, who is seventy-five, get in their car and drive five or six hours to hear me preach. When I stand up to take my text, I look down at my parents and think these are the people who knew me when I was getting a whipping every day because I couldn't stay out of trouble. I remember one summer I asked God, "Please give me one day this summer when I don't get a whipping." That was one of the many prayers that God answered no to.

These are the people who knew me when I flunked algebra, and my mama was an algebra teacher. These are the people (and I'm standing up to take my text looking down at them) who knew me when I played hookie from high school. You know why I got caught? My daddy was the substitute teacher in my English class.

We had a ritual every night at the dinner table. My parents wouldn't say, "How was school today?" If you ask your children that, they can get off real easy — "Fine." One word, and you go on with the rest of your life. But my parents would ask, "What did you do in school today?" and they'd start with the first period and work all the way to the last period.

They would ask my sister first because she was the older, and she would go from first period through gym, and all the way up through the last period. "What did you read in study hall?"

Then they came to me. Daddy said, "And you, young man?" We started in first period and talked about history. Then we talked about math. We went on and got to English. He said, "What did you do in English?" I said, "We're doing Shakespeare."

He said, "Oh, I like Shakespeare. What are you doing, his plays or his poetry?"

"Oh, we're doing his plays." He said, "Which play are you on?"

"*Midsummer Night's Dream*." He said, "No, that was yesterday. We're on *All's Well That Ends Well* today." Another whipping.

These are the people who knew me when. I stand up to take my text and look down at them. These are the people who knew me when the police came to arrest me for grand larceny auto theft at fifteen. These are the people who knew me when I was an embarrassment to them. These are the people who knew me when I broke their hearts and quit school. My granddaddy and my grandmama, who were born as children of slaves and who had no money, graduated from Virginia Union when it was called Hartshorn College and Waylamoy Seminary. My mama and my daddy didn't have any money either. My daddy would work a semester, go to school a semester, and he came out with at B.Th., a B.A., an M.Div., and S.T.M. And here I was with my folks paying for school, and I quit like a dummy and went into the military. These are the people I hurt by my own hard-headedness, my own stubbornness, my own stupidity, and I look down at them as I'm getting ready to take my text. They're sitting there smiling and grinning and crying and praising God, and saying, "That's my child. My child made some mistakes. Oh, but my child is more than those mistakes. You just watch what my child can do."

God's perspective helps us to see things, to see situations, to see our problems, and to see our lives in a different light. There is a way of breaking the cycle of pain and of moving forward with our lives. And the first step on this path to wholeness is to use God's perspective.

Breaking the Cycle of Pain with God's Power

The next step is to use God's power. A lot of the time we can't let go of our past mistakes, failures, hurts, and problems because we're trying to do it on our own strength, under our own power, and we do not have the power to do that. We need to use God's power. I have shared with our congregation and have had them read one of the most beautiful stories I've ever heard in my life. Betty Malz had an ordinary marriage. She was in the church and her husband was not. He wasn't a bad man; he just wasn't in the church. They had an ordinary marriage and they had one child. And then, about seven or eight years into the marriage, her husband got saved. Betty said that everything changed in the marriage. The man started leading devotions at home. Jesus was in their marriage at home. She said the Lord was in their lovemaking and plan making; the Lord was in their arguments and make-ups. His salvation just changed everything.

She became pregnant again, and then, all of a sudden in the third month of her pregnancy, the Lord took her husband home, and she was mad at God. Don't you know that our problems will either drive us to the church or away from the church, to the Lord or away from the Lord? Hers were driving her away. She didn't want to hear anything about God. She didn't want to hear anything about the church. She did not know why God would give her such sadness.

Anger is one of the stages of grief, and she was mad at the Lord. She didn't want to hear any music. She didn't want to hear secular music, because that reminded her of her life with her husband. She didn't want to hear church music, because that reminded her of how he had turned around and how they used to sing church songs at home. The problem was that she had this little daughter who was now eight, and children love music. So she had to work a compromise with her daughter. She said, "I'll tell you what we'll do, honey. Until mommy adjusts and until after the baby comes and mommy's nerves get better, we're not going to have any music at the house, but we will allow music in the car." (And you know how kids are when they're riding down the street in your car. As soon as one song is over, they push the button to another station to hear that song.) The child agreed, "OK, in the car only, but not at home." And that was the compromise they worked out.

One day after picking her child up, Betty stopped by the grocery store to purchase one or two items. On the way home the radio started playing a popular song. This was long before the days of Luther Vandross. It was Dionne Warwick singing "A chair is still a chair even when there's no one sitting there." She didn't want to hear that. She did not want to hear that song because she knew when she climbed the stairs and turned that key, there would be no one there waiting for her. She was rushing to get home so that she could get that key out of the ignition and turn that song off. And, trying not to let her daughter see her cry, she kept her head averted, looking out of the left window. She pulled into the driveway and tried to take the key out of the ignition, but her daughter said, "Mommy, I want to listen." Betty said, "Let's go." Not looking back at her daughter, she reached to grab the bag of groceries but couldn't see that her daughter had taken the bag and was pulling it from the other side. They got into that tug of war that happens momentarily when two people are trying to pick something up at the same time. And in the middle of that tug of war, her little daughter said to her, "Mommy, I can take it, but I can't take it if you won't turn it loose."

Betty said that in the voice of an eight-year-old child she heard the Lord saying to her, "Betty, I can take it, but I can't take it if you won't turn it loose. I can carry it, but I can't carry it if you won't let it go." She said she had been trying to carry that burden all by herself, and the Lord couldn't take it because she would not let it go.

We don't turn it loose, either. We need God's power to turn it loose. We don't have the power to do what God can do. In that hymn "Just a Closer Walk with Thee," the songwriter says, "I am weak, but Thou art strong."

Joseph was able to let go of the hurt, anger, resentment, pain, and self-pity not only because he used God's perspective, but also because he used God's power. He did not rely on his own strength; he relied on the one who increases strength. He relied on the one who has all power in his hand.

His daddy Jacob used to talk about what God had asked his grandfather: "Is anything too hard for the LORD?"[6] So Joseph relied on God's power, and it moved him from the pit of pain and the prison of self-pity into a palace of possibility, which enabled him to say like the apostle Paul, "I can do all things through him who strengthens me."[7] It's God's grace, not mine.

There is a way of breaking the cycle of pain and moving forward with our lives – first by using God's perspective and seeing things as God sees them; next, by using God's power and letting go and letting God. Stop trying to carry it yourself and let God carry it.

Breaking the Cycle of Pain with God's Prescription

Using what I call God's prescription is ultimately the way of breaking the pain cycle. God has given us a prescription for getting unstuck and letting go of that which we say we can't let go of, that which is keeping us back and preventing us from being what God would have us be.

What is God's prescription? Come here, Solomon. Tell us what prescription God gave you. "As [a man] thinketh in his heart, so is he."[8] Watch what you're carrying around in your mind.

What is God's prescription? Come here, Isaiah. Which prescription did God give to you? "Thou dost keep him in perfect peace, whose mind is stayed on thee."[9] Watch what you're carrying around in your mind.

What is God's prescription? Come here, Paul. What prescription did God give you? Paul said, "Well, He gave me two. One is a PRN prescription. That's whenever it's necessary. The other one is a TID[10] prescription: three times a day, every day. Well, what's the PRN prescription, Paul? "Do not worry about anything, but in everything by prayer and supplication with thanksgiving let your requests be made known to God. And the peace of God, which surpasses all understanding, will guard your hearts and your minds in Christ Jesus."[11] Watch what you're carrying around in your mind.

"Finally, beloved, whatever is true, whatever is honorable, whatever is just, whatever is pure, whatever is pleasing, whatever is commendable, if there is any excellence and if there is anything worthy of praise, think about these things."[12] Watch what you're carrying around in your mind. That's the PRN.

Well, what's the other prescription, Paul? What's the TID that you take three times a day, every day? "Beloved, I do not consider that I have made it my own; but this one thing I do: forgetting what lies behind. . . ." Watch what you're carrying around in your mind. Joseph had to forget, or he would have been stuck right there in the pit where his brothers put him. "Forgetting what lies behind and straining forward to what lies ahead, I press on toward the goal for the prize of the heavenly call of God in Christ Jesus."[13]

And here is where that title of this sermon comes in. A ministerial colleague of mine in the A.M.E. Zion church was bringing his daughter home to Chicago after four years of college at Hampton University. When he took her to Hampton, all it took was a couple of suitcases, a footlocker, and two garment bags. But after four years at Hampton, three on campus and one in her own off-campus apartment, she had accumulated so much stuff that when it was time for her to come home, he had to drive down to Hampton, rent a trailer, and load it up with four years of accumulation to bring back to Chicago.

His car had made that trip down and back on several occasions with no problems—Thanksgiving time, Christmas break, summer break—climbing up through those mountains on Highway 70 in Maryland and Pennsylvania, making a journey up the Allegheny Valley through Breezewood, onto the Pennsylvania Turnpike, into Ohio, Indiana. That was nothing when all he had in his car were his passengers and a couple of suitcases. But he discovered that with that trailer hitched on, they had a serious problem in terms of being able to get home.

When they started up those same mountains that they had climbed so many times before, they found that the trailer, loaded down with four years of accumulated stuff, was too much for the little car's engine. My friend said at first he started telling his daughter that story about the little engine that said, "I think I can, I think I can, I think I can."[14] He said, "Well, that worked in the storybook, "but it didn't work with his Honda Civic. The trailer caused them to go slower and slower, and then a storm arose at about the same time that the hill became real steep, and the trailer brought them to a dead stop. He was on the verge of burning out his engine when a state trooper pulled up and told them what to do. The trooper said, "Well, the only way you're going to make it is to unhitch the trailer."

His daughter began protesting immediately on account of her many belongings, and even my friend began thinking of all the money he had invested in that four years of accumulation, and he began protesting. But the trooper said, "You only have two choices: stay here in the storm and fix your car so it can't go anywhere or unhitch the trailer and go on to safety."

Unhitch the Trailer

Paul had to unhitch the trailer: years of accumulated hurt, pain, rejection, and disappointment. Mark left him.[15]

Barnabas fell out with him.[16] Demas cared more about
money than ministry.[17] Paul said, "Forget that. Unhitch the
trailer. Too much stuff will keep me back. I have to press
on."

Joseph had to unhitch the trailer: all of those years of accumulated hurt and not being liked because of how he had
been born and because of what God had given him. All of
that hatred at the hands of his loved ones along with the
experiences of being forgotten about and lied on and messed
over amounted to an accumulation of junk in the trailer of
his memory. But he said, "No, no, no. Unhitch the trailer
and move on."

Out of the storm I had to unhitch the trailer. When my
"best" friend told me the truth that night at the Marine bar-
racks, I said, "I'm not going to let this man see me cry." I
was twenty-one years old. When he left, I cried all night
long. But early in the morning, the Holy Ghost said to me,
"Don't let other folks' problems be your problem. You have
enough of your own without picking up and carrying around
somebody else's. Unhitch the trailer. Let it go."

Somebody has a whole bunch of stuff in the trailer that
you've been dragging around. You need to unhitch. You
have regret. Unhitch it. You have remorse. Unhitch it. You
have disappointment. Unhitch it. I'm not a state trooper,
but I am a soul trooper. And I want you to know that you're
not going to get home trying to drag the trailer. Let it go.
Let it go. Unhitch it.

You want to know how to unhitch? Stop thinking about
way back when and ask one question: What time is it? What
time is it? It's right now. That's what time it is, and the
Lord is blessing me right now. He woke me up this morning
and started me on my way. The Lord is blessing me right
now.

Some of us have things we've been carrying around for
twenty years, twenty-five years. Let them go.

Let us pray:
Father God, we are here in the name of Jesus to do some
unhitching. We have some past hurts we've been carrying

around for five years, ten years, fifteen years, and we need to unhitch them. We have some wrongs that have been done to us, things we did not deserve. We've been nursing and licking wounds and carrying them around and feeling sorry. Lord, we come to unhitch and let them go.

We have some mistakes that we've made that we have not been able to let you take out of our hands. We've been trying to tow them ourselves. God, we come to unhitch. Somebody needs a special anointing.

Some of us need to feel you lifting a burden off of our shoulders. Somebody needs you in his or her life. Lord, while we're down here praying, we ask that you bless right now. Anoint with your Holy Spirit that somebody can be freed up from that which has been tying and holding him or her up and keeping that person from running on to see what the end will be. Lord, we ask it in the name of Jesus. And we thank you in advance in the name of Jesus, because we know you are a God who promised to meet us at the point of need, and we've got some needs tonight, Lord, in terms of letting go of some stuff that has been choking and killing us.

Lord, we're here to thank you in the name of Jesus, because we're going to let it go this time and let you have it. We realize that we can't carry it and you can't carry it if we won't let it go. Lord, we're going to let you take it tonight, and we thank you right now, in the name of Jesus. Praise God!

Study Questions

1. In what ways can the church model a society whose members accept differences in appearance, talents, and backgrounds, as well as other differences?

2. Recall a personal situation or one that you've heard about in which you were unjustly prejudiced toward some-

one because of reasons that person could not help. How did you overcome prejudice? If you did not overcome it, how could you overcome it now?

3. Joseph was victimized by jealousy, backlash because of his own sense of right, and indifference. These experiences could have made him a bitter man. Review these three experiences. Give present examples of how jealousy, indifference, and backlash perpetuate evil in our society.

4. Joseph overcame the temptation to get even by grasping God's perspective on his situation. What was his response to his worried brothers? Can we apply this perspective to injustice in our lives, or is it appropriate at times to "get even"?

5. It has been said that the best revenge is success. Is this a positive way to "get even"? Can anything positive come from a revenge motive?

6. Consider the example of parents who, though they know the past faults of their children, can celebrate their present achievements. How can we apply their example to encourage people who are failing and to welcome back to or into the fold people who have changed for the better? Why is it devastating for the church to hold a long memory of its members' sins? (See John 8:3-11.) Why is it helpful for church leaders to publicly proclaim their own conversions?

7. Joseph's grandfather Abraham was asked by God "Is anything too hard for God?" (Genesis 18:14) Reread the story of Abraham and Sarah as it relates to this question. Think of faith stories in the lives of your family or others that demonstrate the awesome power of God.

8. What are some things that we need to unhitch in our personal, community, church, and national lives?

9. How can we practice "forgetting what lies behind"

(Philippians 3:13) so that we may unhitch our burdensome baggage?

10. "What time is it?" is a critical question and one that is useful for everyday living. Look at this question along with Matthew 6:11, Psalm 118:24, Lamentations 3:22-23, and Philippians 3:13-14. How can these Scriptures help us to live freely in the present and with hope for the future?

What's in This for Me?

Isaiah 43:1-5; Matthew 19:25-30

At the Seminary Consortium for Urban Pastoral Education in the city of Chicago, I teach the history of theology
and the worship experience of the African church in the
North American diaspora.[1] I stress North America because
of the miseducation that leaves most of us unaware of the
fact that there are thirty million Africans living in the diaspora in North America.[2] Another thirty million Africans are
living in Central America and the Caribbean, as well as
sixty million living in South America. We are focusing on
the history of the church in North America. I teach about
our music and our ministers, our origins and our develop-
ment, our pride and our problems, where we have been and
where we are going.

Most of my students at the Seminary Consortium already are pastors or have been placed at urban sites where
they will work for a year as interns or assistants. One of my
students, a young man in his first pastorate who was doing
a fantastic job pastoring a Southern Baptist church, called
me long distance and asked, "Does life in this piranha bowl
[he didn't call it a fish bowl] ever get any better? Is it always
this bad? Does it ever change? Does the mess ever let up?
Do people ever stop being petty? Does the gossip ever go
away? Do the personal attacks ever ease off?" He said, "Dr.
Wright, you've been pastoring four times as long as I have.
Tell me. Is it always this bad? And is this what I said yes to
in serving as a pastor?"

As I listened to my student, I heard at least three things. First, I heard myself posing the same questions across the years—questions that I still ask from time to time, questions about the perils and pitfalls of pastoring. How is it when you're pastoring that you can't get to the people in trouble because of the troublesome people? First I heard questions that I had asked. I heard myself as I listened to my student.

Second, I heard questions that I have heard asked all over this country. Christians and church members have asked me, "How come ever since I joined the church, everything has seemed to go wrong—the bottom done fell out?"

"How come when you try to do right, everything in the world seems to go wrong? You take two steps forward, and you get knocked back three."

"Why is it," some asked me, "that when I was in the world I didn't have these problems?"

One woman said, "Reverend, don't you know that my husband and I had a perfect marriage, and the stronger my faith got, the weaker the bonds of matrimony got?"

"How come this thing don't work out like the Bible says it's supposed to work out? What is God trying to tell me?"

"Does it ever get any better? Is it always this bad?"

"I got children to raise," one woman said, "and they need a daddy and they ain't got none. What am I supposed to do, and where is God when I need God? I go to church and it don't do no good. I'm still catchin' hell and I don't understand."

"If God is so powerful," another asked, "why am I still having problems?"

One churchman, trying to stay in Christ, caught his wife in bed with an officer of the church. Another man, who was a hard-working, God-fearing church member, watched in agony as his wife died in her thirties from a brain aneurysm. And he asked me, "Reverend, what kind of God does this?"

My son in the ministry and his wife lived through a tragedy that almost defies description. She carried a baby for nine months in her womb only to watch in grief as the baby died after less than six hours on this earth. "What is the

Lord doing?" they asked me. "Does it ever let up? Is it always this bad?"

As I listened to my student on the phone that night, I heard questions that I have asked myself, and I heard questions that Christians all over the country have asked me. And then I heard the question that Peter asked in this passage.

I often tell my congregation that Peter is my favorite disciple—bold, brash, brave, and at times a brazen brother. Whatever Peter did, he did it whole hog. When he was right, Peter was all the way right. And when he was wrong, Peter was all the way wrong. Whether walking on the water, or humbugging in the garden, or cussin' in the courtyard, Peter did not half-step at anything. And there are times, I'm convinced, that when Peter opened his mouth, he was speaking for a lot of us.

Many of Jesus' followers became dissatisfied with his discourse and left him. Isn't it funny how when folk get mad at God's message, they walk away from God's messenger? Folk were walking away, and Jesus asked the Twelve, "Would you also like to leave?" And Peter spoke up, "Lord, to whom would we go? You have the words that give eternal life" (John 6:66-68, GNB).

We Need His Words

When Peter opened his mouth, he was speaking for a lot of us. We need the words of Jesus. We cannot live without the words of Jesus. Where else could we go to hear "Come unto me all ye that labour and are heavy laden, and I will give you rest" (Matthew 11:28, KJV)? Where else can we go to hear somebody say "I am the bread of life. I am the good shepherd. I am the way, the truth, and the life"?[3]

We need his words when we're lonely: "Lo, I am with you alway even unto the end of the world" (Matthew 28:20, KJV). We need his words when we're picked on: "Blessed are ye, when men shall revile you, and persecute you, and say all manner of evil against you falsely, for my sake. Rejoice and be exceeding glad . . ." (Matthew 5:11-12, KJV). We need his words when we're falling and when we're failing: "If you re-

main in me and my words remain in you, then you will ask
for anything you wish, and you shall have it" (John 15:7,
GNB). We need his words when we gather to worship:
"Where two or three are gathered in my name, there am I in
the midst of them" (Matthew 18:20, RSV). We need his
words when we're weak: "My grace is sufficient for you" (2
Corinthians 12:9, RSV).

Peter Spoke for Us

Where else can we go to get words like his words? Peter
said, "Lord, to whom would we go? You have the words that
give eternal life." When he opened his mouth, Peter was often speaking for a lot of us.

Out in the middle of a storm when one appeared saying,
"Don't be afraid," Peter spoke up, "Lord, if it's really you,
order me to come out on the water to you" (Matthew 14:27-
28, RSV). In other words, in the midst of a storm, give me
some proof that it's really you.

On the Mount of Transfiguration,[4] church got so good it
couldn't get no "gooder." Things were so hot that heaven
opened up and came down to earth, bringing a little bit of
its essence along. And when that service got to really smok-
ing, Peter spoke up. "Lord! Great God from Zion! It's just
good to be here!"

When the Lord said those who loved him would leave him,
Peter spoke up. "Not me, Lord. Not the kid. I'm ready to go
to prison and die with you" (Matthew. 26:31-35, author's
paraphrase). "Wherever the Lord leads, I'll follow" is what
we say. When Peter opened his mouth, I have a feeling that
he was speaking for a lot of us, even when he denied who he
was and whose he was to save his own skin.[5] That is no more
than what we do on a day-to-day basis, up to and including
the cussin' part.

On the coast of Caesarea Philippi, when Jesus said, "Who
do men say that I am?" the disciples said, "Some say Elijah.
Some say Jeremiah. Some say Isaiah" (Matthew 16:13-14,
author's paraphrase). But when Jesus asked his next question, "But who do you say that I am?" Peter spoke up: "You

are the Christ, the Son of the living God" (Matthew 16:15-16, GNB). He confessed his faith like we confess our faith. When Peter opened his mouth, he spoke for many of us.

Jesus said, "If another member of the church sins against you, go and point out the fault when the two of you are alone" (Matthew 18:15, NRSV). Peter spoke up. "Lord, how many times do I have to forgive him or her? Seven? Let's put a cap on this thing somewhere" (author's paraphrase). [And this has been my question across the years: How do you heal an open wound?] When Peter opened his mouth, he was speaking for a lot of us. So it is not a surprise that when Peter speaks in Matthew 19, I can hear us. And when my student pours out his soul to me long distance, I can hear Peter. Verse 27 says that Peter spoke up once more.

What's in This for Me?

Jesus had just had a disturbing dialogue with a young man who had all of the symbols of success on the outside and all of the symptoms of emptiness and failure on the inside. On the outside the young man was rich, but on the inside he was bankrupt. On the outside he had money, but on the inside he was miserable.

On the outside he looked like he had what everyone else would want, but on the inside he felt like he wanted what everyone else seemed to have. He was in the church and empty. He was among the saints and still seeking. Sounds like some of us, doesn't he? He was young with his whole life ahead of him, yet he felt that he somehow had missed what life was really all about.

We've got us a five- or six-figure-per-annum buppie in Matthew 19, with "money's mammy" and misery. He came to Jesus. He started off right. But it's not how you start off; it's how you end up. He wanted to hear what the Lord had to say, but he did not want to do what the Lord said to do. Sounds like a lot of us, doesn't it?

He had sense enough to try Jesus, but not faith enough to trust Jesus. So he went away sad because what he had, had him. His loot was more important to him than his life.

What he made was more important than the one who made him. What he had in stash for himself meant more to him than what the Lord had in store for him.

Jesus watched a yuppie sell his soul for some compound interest, give up a mansion in glory for some stuff that he couldn't take with him "nohow," give up what he could have for that which he couldn't really ever have. Jesus watched that and said, "It is much harder for a rich person to enter the Kingdom of God than for a camel to go through the eye of a needle" (19:24, GNB) or for a Cadillac to go through a revolving door.

At the time the disciples were hearing this, the biggest thing they had seen in Palestine was a camel; the smallest thing was a needle. When the disciples heard this, they were so startled that they started asking, "Who, then, can be saved?" (19:25, GNB).

Jesus gave one of his usual deep answers. "This is impossible for man, but for God everything is possible" (19:26, GNB). A disturbing dialogue, a deep answer, and that was it!

Peter had had it. So Peter spoke up, "Look, Lord. I don't understand. We have left everything and followed you. Now what will we have?" (19:27, author's paraphrase).

"What's in this for us? What's in this for me? You know, I've got a wife in Capernaum to think about, a mother-in-law, and a family. Now where is this thing heading? You keep talking about Calvary and a crucifixion. What are you trying to tell me?

"Does it ever get any better? Is it always this bad? How come since I joined up with you everything done gone wrong? My daddy's business done fell off. And Andrew and I had a good thing in this fishing business, but we left fishing and went to following, and my wife is sick of it. Following don't put food on the table like fishing does. My mother-in-law is on my case. I'm taking a big risk here. And I got little or nothing to show for it. What am I gonna have? What's in this for me? When does it get better? When does the trouble stop and the triumph start?

"I ain't rich like that young ruler, but I was doing all right by myself. I left it, I followed you, and I ain't seen nothin' but hard times since I started.

"Folks wanted to kill us in Jerusalem, and if you think I'm going to give up my sword, you got another think coming. You almost got yourself lynched in Nazareth with that fool sermon you preached.

"The Samaritans don't want us. The Galileans asked us to leave their territory. They were more interested in saving pigs than saving people. The Pharisees don't like us. The Sadducees ain't too happy about us. The scribes are hot under the collar. Herod is mad at you, and your own family thinks you're kind of touched in the head.

"Now look! We done give up a lot, and for what? Does it ever get any better? Is it always this bad? What will we have when the deal goes down? What's in this for me? The rich young ruler wouldn't follow you, but we have. There must be some kind of reward – something going. Tell me what it is! I decided to follow you and I said yes, yet everything seems to go wrong."

Peter and my students are saying in different ways the same thing: What's in this for me? And when Peter speaks, he speaks for a lot of us. We might not be so bold as to say to the Lord, "Now look, Lord," but sometimes, somewhere inside of us, that nagging question returns: What is the point? Why am I doing this? Where is the payoff? What about me? I'm getting my head whipped and I don't understand. Somebody tell me something.

The Lord Answers—The Lord Promises

When you ask the Lord a question, the Scriptures show that the Lord will always answer. We may not like the answer. We may not understand the answer. We may disagree with the answer. We may not hear the answer sometimes. We may even miss the answer. But when you ask the Lord a question as a believer, Scripture shows us that the Lord will always answer.

Let's look at the answer he gave Peter, because his answer to Peter is also his answer to us. When Peter asked, "What will we have?" Jesus first made Peter a promise. He said,

"You can be sure . . ." (Matthew 19:28, GNB). Promises are problematic for a lot of us. We don't do too well with promises, and we don't put too much stock in promises. We have promised so much and been promised so much and have seen those promises broken so many times that we don't put much stock in promises.

The broken promises in our lives are not only promises that other people have made to us; sometimes they are promises that we have made to ourselves. We promised to pay our car note on time. We promised to support our church and pay our tithes. We promised to serve him until we die. We promised to pay VISA, MasterCard, and American Express on time. We promised so many things: "I won't tell a soul. No one has to know. . . . Girl, let me tell you."

We promised, some of us, to always love and never be untrue. We promised, "Lord, if you'll just help me this one time, I promise I won't do it no more." Some of us have promised to love, honor, cherish, and obey until death do us part, and we have promised that two or three times.

Promises don't mean that much. We don't put that much stock in promises because we have seen them broken. But when Peter asked this question (which is also our question), he hears the promise. And the Lord's promises are not like our promises. You see, when the Lord makes a promise, he doesn't come short of his word. There is no gap between what he says and what he will do.

He promised a Wonderful Counselor, and he kept that promise. He promised a Mighty God, and he kept that promise. He promised an Everlasting Father, and he kept that promise. He promised a Prince of Peace, and he kept that promise. (See Isaiah 9:6.)

He promised that "If you tear this building down, I'll raise it up again in three days" (John 2:19, author's paraphrase), and he kept that promise. He promised "If I be lifted up from the earth, I'll draw all men, women, boys and girls unto me" (John 12:32, author's paraphrase). Didn't he draw you? He kept that promise?

He promised never to leave me, never to leave me alone. He promised that weeping may endure for a night, but joy is coming in the morning. He promised to be a doctor in a sick room, a lawyer in a courtroom, to be a presence in the prayer room. He promised to be a mother for the motherless and a father for the fatherless. And whatever he promised, he's already done.

When the Lord makes a promise, it's already done. How did Peter put it? The Lord is not slack concerning his promise. The Lord makes what I like to call a holy promise. That's the difference between his and ours. When Peter asked his question, the first thing the Lord did was to make a holy promise.

Not Only Promises, But Problems

The second thing that struck me, especially as I listened to my student's question, and to my question, and to yours (Does it ever get any better?), was this: What's in this for me? for us? Not only a holy promise, but some human problems. When you look at Mark's account of this question (Mark 10:30), Jesus says clearly, you'll receive a hundred times more houses, a hundred times more brothers and sisters, a hundred times more mothers and children, a hundred times more things and possessions in this life, plus you're going to receive a hundred times more persecution as well. In other words, along with the blessings, you're also going to have some human problems.

A lot of us get tricked by some of the new thought theology that promises only prosperity and no adversity. Well, that's cute, but that is not Christianity. Jesus said, "You're going to have some persecution. You're going to have some problems. You're going to have some troubles, trials and tribulations in the world. This world is going to make you suffer. But hold on anyway. Be of good cheer, because I have overcome the world" (John 16:33, author's paraphrase).

You're going to have some human problems: homes that are less than perfect, churches that are less than perfect, and relationships that are less than perfect. Those homes, churches, and relationships have imperfect people in them, don't they? You're there, aren't you? Then how do you think it's going to be perfect? A lot of people try to run away from their problems, but you can't run, because wherever you go, you're taking some with you.

God's Heavenly Presence

Because we're going to have some human problems, I am glad that the final word, the Lord's answer, doesn't end with a problem. There's another word that he gives us, and it is found in verse 28, where he says that he will be with those who have followed him. In other words, what he guarantees is a heavenly presence. It's the same thing Isaiah 43 says. You're not only going to have holy promises and some human problems, but when you pass through deep waters (those are human problems), I'll be with you (heavenly presence). Your troubles will not overwhelm you. When you pass through fire (human problems), I'll be with you (a heavenly presence). When hard trials come (human problems), I'll be with you (heavenly presence). The Lord's name means Emmanuel: God is with us. And when you've got human problems, you've also got the heavenly presence of the problem solver. His presence is a foretaste of glory divine.

What's in this for me? What's in this for you? Holy promises, human problems, and the heavenly presence of the problem solver.

One song in our church says, "Makes no difference what the problem, I can go to God in prayer." You got a personal problem? Just say, "in the name of Jesus." Charles Walker was telling Bill Jones[6] and me about a fellow who got saved at the bus stop when he tried to snatch a woman's purse. The old sister just said, "Jesus!" When he reached back to hit her, she said, "Jesus!" Then he tried to hit her again. She said, "Jesus!" He let go of the purse and grabbed hold of Christ, saved at the bus stop because of Jesus. In the name of Jesus. Just calling his name brings a little bit of heaven into your life no matter what that situation is.

The Biblical Testimony to Heaven

Trinity Church is an unusual church. We have Dr. Jawanza Kunjufu, one of the foremost educators and black nationalist Christians in the country. We've got former

Muslims who are members of our church. We've got some folk who left the Kemetic religion[7] and Jacob Carruthers.[8] In fact, Carruthers' former wife is an active member in our church; the wife of Dr. Bobby Wright, eminent black psychologist, is a member of our church. We've got some folks who come out of that strong left-wing African American Afrocentrism, and when I start talking about heaven, they get nervous. Plus, we've got some intellectuals in our church, some good old United Church of Christ folk who come out of the Congregational tradition, and they don't like for folks with academic degrees to talk about heaven, because that's so primitive, you see. And some of that's true. So much that passes itself off as black religion is so heavenly focused that it does no earthly good. But I tell my educated friends and my nationalist friends that I cannot completely drop heaven from my preaching. You don't get rid of the baby in the bath just because the bath water's dirty. I know some of my educated friends and nationalist friends and conscious friends[9] do not like for me to preach about heaven. When I say "heavenly presence," they sort of cringe. They feel that it's primitive and beneath my dignity and my degrees.

But I say to my nationalist friends and to my educated friends, don't try to make me do away with heaven. If I drop heaven, I'm going to lose the first verse in my Bible: "In the beginning God created the heavens and the earth."

If I drop heaven, I'm going to lose two of my Ten Commandments, the second and the fourth. Number two says, "Thou shalt not make unto thee any graven image of any likeness of any thing that is in heaven above, or that is in the earth beneath." And number four says, "Remember the sabbath day, to keep it holy . . . For in six days, the LORD made heaven and earth" (Exodus 20:4, 8, 11, KJV).

If I drop heaven, I'm going to have to stop saying Psalm 121: "I will lift up mine eyes unto the hills, from whence cometh my help. My help cometh from the LORD, which made heaven and earth" and Psalm 139: "Whither shall I go from thy spirit? or whither shall I flee from thy presence? If I ascend up into heaven, thou art there."

If I drop heaven, I'm going to have to stop quoting Isaiah 66:1: "Thus saith the LORD, The heaven is my throne, and the earth is my footstool."

If I drop heaven, I'm going to have to throw away John the Baptist's sermon: "Repent, for the kingdom of heaven is at hand" (Matthew 3:2).

If I get rid of heaven, I'm going to have to get rid of what happened when Jesus was baptized, and the spirit of God descended like a dove, and lo a voice from heaven said "This is my beloved Son, in whom I am well pleased" (Matthew 3:16-17, KJV).

If I drop heaven, I'm going to have to stop saying the Beatitudes. The first one says, "Blessed are the poor in spirit: for theirs is the kingdom of heaven." The last one says, "Rejoice, and be exceeding glad: for great is your reward in heaven" (Matthew 5:3,12, KJV).

If I drop heaven, I'm going to have to stop praying my favorite prayer, "Our Father, which art in heaven, Hallowed be thy name" (Matthew 6:9,KJV).

If I drop heaven, I'm going to have to stop saying one of my favorite verses of Scripture: "If my people, which are called by my name, shall humble themselves, and pray, and seek my face, and turn from their wicked ways; then will I hear from heaven, and will forgive their sin, and will heal their land" (2 Chronicles 7:14, KJV).

If I drop heaven, I'm going to have to do away with the Second Coming; I'm going to have to get rid of Pentecost. I'm going to have to throw Revelation out of my Bible.

If I drop heaven, I'm going to have to break some dates, because I've got a grandmama there and a grandfather there, and I promised them I would meet them in heaven. If I drop heaven, I'm going to have to stop singing a whole lot of songs that are my favorite songs, like, "Oh, I want to see him, look upon his face. Home at last, cares all past. . . ." I'm going to have to stop singing "Beams of heaven as I go." I'm going to have to stop singing, "Walk around heaven all day." I'm going to have to stop singing, "When we all get to heaven what a day of rejoicing that will be."

Don't make me drop heaven.

Beams of heaven as I go,
Thro' this wilderness below,
Guide my feet in peaceful ways,
Turn my midnights into days;

When in the darkness I would grope,
Faith always sees a star of hope,
And soon from all life's griefs and danger,
I shall be free some day.

I do not know how long 'twill be,
Nor what the future holds for me,
But this I know, if Jesus leads me,
I shall get home some day.[10]

Study Questions

1. The term *diaspora* refers to black descendants of Africa who live in other parts of the world. Discuss the definition of "diaspora" and its concept as it applies to helping North American blacks form a positive view of their heritage, as well as their connection (cultural, spiritual, economic, historical) to people of African descent throughout the world.

2. Reflect on the part of this sermon that points to our need for the words of Jesus. Can you make a list of five of Jesus' phrases that have special meaning for you?

3. Choose two examples of Peter's comments from the sermon section "Peter Spoke for Us" or other examples from the Bible. Tell how Peter speaks for you in these examples.

4. Describe the difference in just trying Jesus and in having the faith to trust Jesus.

5. The answer to, What's in this for me? is God's promises and presence, and life's problems. Look at some of the

promises that God makes, as mentioned in the sermon. Relate one of them to a community, national, or international situation of which you are aware.

6. In what ways have you seen the evidence of God's heavenly presence during some trial in your life or in the life of someone you know?

7. What's wrong with doctrines that teach us that we won't have problems if we have sufficient faith? What verse of Scripture disputes this claim?

8. In what sense may talk about heaven be "primitive"?

9. How can we incorporate our beliefs about heaven into our religion in a positive way?

10. Have you answered the question, What's in this for me? What is your answer?

When You Forget
Who You Are

Esther 4:11-17
Background Scripture (Esther 2:1-11)

Once there was a girl named Hadassah. Hadassah had a
series of serious problems. First, she was carried away into
captivity like the Africans who would centuries later sail
away from Senegal, never to see nor set foot again on the
soil that gave birth to the world civilizations – the soil that
had fed their families, that had caught their tears, on which
they had fallen in love and made love, the soil into which
they had placed the bodies of parents and grandparents.
Like these African citizens who were taken from their
homes centuries later, never to return, Hadassah (2:6) was
carried away forever into captivity.

First she was taken away from all of the sights, sounds,
scenes, and smells that she knew and loved so much. Second, there was the taking away of her name and her history.
She was no longer Hadassah. As a matter of fact, most
Christians don't even know that Hadassah was her name.
We just know her by her slave name – Esther. Hadassah was
the name she first heard cooed into her consciousness, long
before she could crawl, walk, or talk; Hadassah, the name
that she grew up knowing, hearing, and understanding to be
part and parcel of who she was and whose she was; Hadassah, the name by which her mama called her when she
wanted her to come home, when she wanted her to behave,
when she wanted her to be still, when she wanted her to
hurry up, when she wanted her to shut up; Hadassah, the
name that was said proudly when she took her first steps,

and the name that was said softly when she met her first love. Her captors took her name, Hadassah, away from her and called her Esther.

First they took her away from her home; then they took her name away from her. Next they took her out of the stability of a home and put her in a harem. Her parents had died when she was a child (I told you she had several problems), so she was orphaned at an early age. Abihail, her father, had a nephew whose Hebrew name is not even known or given in this text. He was called Mordecai, his Babylonian or Akkadian name, after the Babylonian God Marduk. Operating on the African principle of the extended family, Mordecai took her in, adopted her, and reared her. She was like his own daughter.

When her home of origin was taken away from her by the death of her parents, Mordecai provided a stable home environment for Hadassah. He gave her somewhere to grow, somewhere to learn love, somewhere to laugh, somewhere to cry. He gave her a place to do homework, to play jacks, to jump Double-Dutch, to share dreams, and to grow strong. Mordecai gave Hadassah a home, and now even that home was taken away from her.

From the warmth and security of a home where she was loved, she was snatched and put into the fast track of a harem, where she was taught how to make love. From an environment of cooperation, she was thrown into a climate of competition. From a place where she was cared about for who she was, she was thrust into a place that only was concerned about what she looked like. Hadassah had a series of serious problems.

They took her away from her homeland. They took her away from her home folks after death had taken her parents away, and then they put her in a harem full of foxes because (according to verse 7) she was a beautiful girl. Hadassah had a series of serious problems. She was moved from her regular place where the other exiles lived in the ghetto (even though it was a nice ghetto with neatly manicured lawns and heavily mortgaged bungalows, just the sort of place where an administrator in the government would live) to the royal palace. She was taken from the care of Mordecai and placed in the care of Hegai. Where Mordecai had charge of the home, Hegai had charge of the harem. Where Mordecai had seen to the care of her well-being, to the condition of her soul, and to her training in the faith of Abraham and Sarah, Isaac and Rebecca, Jacob and Rachel—where Mordecai had seen to her well-being, Hegai saw to her good grooming. Where Mordecai had looked after the condition of her soul, Hegai looked after the condition of her body. Where Mordecai had been concerned about training her in the faith, Hegai was only concerned about training her in the finesse of being a fox. He lost no time, the Word says, in beginning a beauty treatment of massage and a special diet.

The Hebrews already had a special diet that was designed by Moses for the purity of their souls. But Hegai had another special diet that was designed by the masseuses for the shape of her body. Hadassah, I tell you, had a series of serious problems: a training program that ran roughshod over her religious upbringing, beauty treatments and diets that completely ignored the faith in which she had been nourished, and then, on top of that, some questionable advise given to her in terms of owning the Almighty. Mordecai advised Hadassah, or Esther, as she would be called, to keep her Jewish heritage a secret.

Hadassah Had to Keep a Secret

With seven girls assigned to her as her personal round-the-clock servants in the palace, Hadassah had to keep it a secret that she believed in the power of prayer. She had to keep it a secret that she worshiped the One who was called I Am that I Am, the One who spoke and the worlds came into being, the One who stepped off of nowhere onto somewhere and created everywhere, the One who moved off of nothing onto something and made everything. She had to keep it a secret that she prayed to a God who had already asked, "Is anything too hard for the Lord?"[1]

She had to keep it a secret that she called on the same God who put a ram in the bushes for Abraham;[2] the same God who sent a caravan by a pit for Joseph;[3] the same God who took what Joseph's brothers meant for evil and turned it around for good;[4] the same God who constructed a highway in the middle of the Red Sea, making a way out of no way;[5] the same God who made the sun stand still over Gibeon until the battle was fought and the victory won.[6] She had to keep it a secret that she called on the same God who sent down a fiery chariot for Elijah;[7] the same God who closed up a lion's mouth for Daniel;[8] the same God who got in a fiery furnace to hold a prayer vigil with Shadrach, Meshach, and Abednego;[9] the same God who was like fire shut up in Jeremiah's bones;[10] that same God – she had to keep it a secret.

Hadassah Became Esther

So she gave up her spiritual habits in order to pick up some new sexual habits. Whenever somebody asks you to give up your God in exchange for something else, watch out! Something terrible is about to happen. No wonder Mordecai walked back and forth every day in front of the courtyard of the harem to see what was going to happen to this girl he had reared like his daughter. Slowly but surely the metamorphosis came. She changed little bit by little bit into a magnificent monster, created by an alien culture. She underwent the Babylonian beauty treatment. The regular beauty treatment for the women lasted for a year: massage with oil of myrrh for six months and then with oil of balsam for six more months (2:12). For one solid year she was given daily massages and daily facials, daily steam baths in the Babylonian spas, and daily mud packs in the royal Babylonian beauty salons.

She was already fine. But Hegai saw to it that they did it "to the max": L'Oreal, Estee Lauder, Mary Kay, Fashion Fair, Bourghese, Clinique, and Perscriptives; cinnamon bronze Babylonian base, strawberry red Babylonian blush; eye liner and eye shadow, eyebrow pencil and lip pencil, mascara and lip gloss, and just a hint of deep translucent pressed powder. Manicures and pedicures. Genteel permanent. Optimum neutralizing shampoo. TCB protein conditioner. Kintex moisturizing conditioner. Twenty minutes under the dryer, a combout, and just a hint of Cartier or Kritzia. Hegai gave them a choice (2:13) of a Bill Blass negligee or a Christian Dior teddy. As M.C. Hammer would say, "You can't touch that!"

Slowly but surely the transformation took place. She was transformed from the mild-mannered lass that Mordecai knew to the sexiest siren in Xerxes' estate.[11] And Mordecai kept walking back and forth in front of the courtyard to see what was happening to this lass he told to lie about the Lord.

Esther Married a Foolish King

Hegai was pleased with what he saw, but Mordecai was mortified with what he saw. Esther had married a man that she did not know and had become queen (2:17) to a king that she did not love. Whenever somebody asks you to give up your God in exchange for what they can get you, watch out! Something terrible is about to happen. This man that she married was a complete fool. Not only did he not share her value system and faith, but he also did not share her culture or her ethical assumptions.

Read chapter 1. Back in chapter 1 this man that she married had given a banquet, a party that lasted a whole week. Drinks were flowing like Niagara Falls. Verse 8 says there was no limit to the drinks. Talk about a happy hour—they had open bar for a whole week, seven days of "gettin' to' down and drunk as a cootie brown." And on the seventh day, when he was out of his head (1:10-11), he said, "Y'all go get Queen Vashti and bring her in here. And tell her to wear her royal crown. I'm gonna show y'all what fine is." Now maybe he meant that she should have nothing on *but* her crown, or maybe it meant she should wear all of her royal finery. Nonetheless, he wanted to parade his wife in front of his drunken guests, and he expected her to obey immediately. He completely ignored her rights as a person and her dignity as an individual, much less her position as the queen of the country. This was the kind of king that Esther married.

He had a harem full of concubines[12] that Esther already knew about. This was no new information that was sprung on her after she was already in the relationship. She walked into this with her eyes wide open, compromising everything she believed in and the way she was reared for what might possibly come her way once she was raised to her new position as queen, first lady of the land. She gave up what she got in the church house for what she might get in the big house or the White House, partially because her cousin told her to do that. Verse 20, chapter 2 (GNB) says, "As for Esther, she had still not let it be known that she was Jewish." Mordecai had told her not to tell anyone, and she obeyed him in this, just as she had obeyed him when she was a little girl under his care."

I don't know if you realize just how much of her culture she had to let go of in order to carry out this deception. But for a Jewish girl, there were not only certain foods she was not supposed to eat, which she was now eating; there were not only certain things that she was not supposed to do, which she was now doing; there were not only certain days that she was supposed to observe as holy days, which she was now ignoring for her 365-day-a-year beauty treatment; but fourteen days out of each month, Jewish girls were supposed to separate themselves from the rest of the people and be with God. She was ignoring that because she was keeping her faith a secret, and slowly but surely the transformation came.

Esther Forgot Who She Was

The deception stopped bothering her. It got to the point, especially when she became queen, that she could out-Babylonian the Babylonians. Assimilation is like that. It slowly kills you. You don't even realize what is happening to you, because when you assimilate, you forget who you are. As a matter of fact, sin and assimilation are just alike. They work the same way an Eskimo kills a wolf. At a United Church of Christ caucus meeting of racial and ethnic minorities, one of the Eskimos told of an ingenious way his culture had developed for killing a wolf. An Eskimo takes his knife, coats the blade with human blood, and lets it freeze. Then he adds another coat of blood and lets it freeze. He adds more and more coats of blood and lets them all freeze until that blade is hidden deep within a substantial thickness of frozen human blood. Then the Eskimo buries the knife in the ice with the blade up and the handle down. The wolf catches a scent of blood and comes over and starts licking. The more feverishly he licks, the more his hot tongue starts melting the frozen blood, and it tastes good. He licks faster and faster and faster until the blade is bare, but he keeps on licking harder and harder, because it's so cold he can't tell that it's his tongue being cut on that blade, and he's swallowing his own life. He doesn't realize that he's satisfying his craving for blood with his own blood. He licks the blade until he bleeds to death, swallowing his own life. And that is how both sin and assimilation work.

When we get a little taste of sin, or we get a little taste of Babylonian culture, the finer things of Babylonian life— Babylonian jewels, Babylonian values, Babylonian labels, Babylonian lifestyle—the little taste we get of sin (or of assimilation) makes us crave more and more. Esther looked good in those Babylonian hairstyles. Esther felt good in that Babylonian silk up against her smooth, soft body. Esther smelled good in that Babylonian perfume. The more we get, the more we crave, and we go deeper and deeper, satisfying our desires. We never notice we are slowly destroying ourselves until it's too late. Only when we are dying do we realize we have swallowed our own life, or been strangled to death by the enemy's life.

This came home for me back in 1979. When I was working on my master's thesis at Howard, I ran across references to blacks off the northern coast of South America in Suriname. The references were always tantalizing, teasing little tidbits that never told you much, but just said, "Unlike the Africans of Suriname, Africans in North America . . ." and would go on to talk about us. And I kept wondering, Who are these blacks in Suriname and what do they do? My question was answered when I bought a great big, fat book entitled *Suppression of the Revolt of the Negroes in Suriname*, which had been reprinted by Greenwood Press. The book was written by the colonel from the Surinamese Dutch colony whose job it was to stop this rebellion. A group of African maroons[13] took over a ship, just as in the Amistad incident in the United States,[14] and had sailed onto the coast of Suriname in South America. Only instead of going off into the bush and escaping, they hung around the village edge, and every time a slave ship would come into port, they would free the slaves. At first I thought the brothers were freedom fighters. As I got into the book further, though, I found out that the brothers weren't freedom fighters at all. On that first ship there were forty-seven men and no women, so the brothers were asking, "What we gonna escape for? What we gonna do with each other?" So every time a ship came in, they would free the slaves in hopes of getting women. When they finally got enough women, they started up in the bush. In the meantime, the Dutch sent over a regiment of their troops to put down the rebellious Negroes from Africa. And the Dutch lost because they fought just like Bill Cosby humorously portrayed the British fighting style in the American Revolution: They all lined up in a straight line in their bright red and blue uniforms, and one rank would kneel and reload while another one fired. While the Dutch practiced this formal European style of war, the Africans were up in the trees easily shooting them down with arrows. So the Dutch lost.

Well, the Dutch signed a treaty with them and gave them their freedom. The Africans were composed of three basic tribal groups out of Ghana, Abidjan, Accra, and Lagos. The Dutch let them have their freedom, and for two hundred years the Africans went up the Amazon and were untouched by Western civilization.

After reading this book, I got so excited that I called Eastern Airlines, Pan Am, and American. I wanted to go see these African brothers and sisters. I found out that the closest I could get was into the city of Suriname; then I would have to charter a pirogue (that's a long-poled boat) and be taken two hundred miles up the Amazon (if I could find two people who could speak the language groupings up there). Then I decided that the Lord didn't want me to spend my vacation that way, so I didn't go on that trip.

But at the same time, to show you how the Lord works, two scholars with Ph.D's from Harvard University, a man named Evans and a man named Counter, had discovered these same people, and they were making preparations to go see them. Some of you who watch public television might have seen their program. It was called "I Sought My Brother."[15] They also published a book that described their trip up the Amazon and their living with the people for six to eight months the first time, and then at six-month intervals at various other times. My congregation, knowing I wanted to go to Suriname, gave me that book for Christmas, and it was like a homecoming. I cherished it. As a matter of fact, each night after I read my Bible, I would get the book out and read ten or fifteen pages and just look at those pictures and savor what it would have been like to be there. When I saw some of the pictures, I was glad I had made that decision not to go, because some branches along the Amazon had boa constrictors wrapped around them. The Lord knew what he was doing in keeping me from going there.

It was New Year's Eve when I read the passage in the book telling about their arrival in the village. Rounding the bend in the Amazon, the lead polist stood up and put his pole down. And Evans said, "Why are you stopping?" The polist said, "We're here."

Evans said, "I don't see anything." The polist replied, "They see us." As they went into the sand, Evans said, "Let's get out." The polist said, "You don't get out and go into their village without permission from the chief. Wait a minute." They could see eyes behind the leaves, and finally the people came out to talk to them. They said, "We would like permission to speak to the chief because we need permission to come into your village."

The chief came forty-five minutes later. (The chief operated on African time.) They began a fascinating dialogue through the translator. The translator said, "These are your brothers from North America." The chief had never heard of North America. "It's many, many miles from here. There are people up there. . . ." The chief was just looking. He couldn't understand. Finally the translator said, "They're looking for their home, their ancestors." That struck a responsive chord because one of the three tribes there is called "The Lost Tribe." The griot (tribal oral historian) had to reach way back into West African history to tell their tribal story. He said that the white devils came, put them in the holds of slave ships, and sailed them around in circles. But they got free. They thought they were home because when you look at a map, you see that Suriname is close in latitude to Ghana; it has the same flora, same fauna, and the same temperatures. Because of this, they thought they were back in Africa; they just didn't know where their village was. That's how the story goes in their oral history.

"Oh yes," said the chief. "We, too, are looking for our home. We, too, are looking for our first village. "So yes," he agreed, "they may come ashore, but before they do, ask them this one question: Have you won your war with the white devil or are you still fighting it?"

And Evans looked at Counter, and Counter looked at Evans, and they said, "I guess we're still fighting ours," to which the chief responded, "If you are fighting it, why do you wear the clothes of the enemy?" And it hit me that night. I closed the book that night, that New Year's Eve, and began weeping, because it dawned on me that if you were to go back to your church tomorrow and ask your folk to give up their Louis Vuitton or Coach[16] . . . that blade is so deep inside of us that most of us don't see ourselves as Africans living in diaspora.[17]

When Esther got to the point that she could practice Babylonian customs more than they did, she forgot who she was. The first issue in the text is this: You can play a role only so long and pretend so long. If you keep on doing it, you're going to take on that role and forget who you are. Keep reading. When Haman tricked the king into signing that death warrant for all the Jews, Mordecai sent word to the queen, who was no longer Hadassah but Queen Esther. Look at how she answered him (4:11, NRSV): "All the king's servants and the people of the king's provinces know that if any man or woman goes to the king inside the inner court without being called, there is but one law – all alike are to be put to death. Only if the king holds out the golden scepter to someone, may that person live. I myself have not been called to come in to the king for thirty days." In other words, "Mordecai, I can't help you. I can't help 'you people.' "

A lot of us don't know this side of Esther. We skip over to "If I perish" (4:16). But Esther, when she was first asked for help, denied Mordecai. She pretended for so long that she had become the role that she was playing. "Nothing I can do about it. Sorry, Mordecai. I can't give up what I got for y'all." She started telling him what was possible, what was plausible, what was feasible, and what was politically expedient, given the parameters of her prerogatives at that particular existential moment in time. Read it. She forgot who she was.

When You Forget, You Think You're Better Than Others

A second issue in this text is that when you forget who you are, you start thinking that you are better than your own people. You start thinking of your own people as "them," not "us." You start thinking of black people as "y'all" and not "we." And once you start thinking like that, you start acting like Esther: like you "is" what you "ain't." That's bad English and good theology.

Malcolm X addressed this issue most powerfully and poignantly more than thirty years ago. Malcolm asked this kind of question: Do you think that when lynch mobs or racists look at you they see a black Baptist, a black Methodist, a black Presbyterian, a black Congregationalist, a black U.C.C.,[18] a black Muslim, a black Democrat, a black Republican, a black Ph.D., a black physician, a black corporate executive? It isn't the word that comes after "black" that has them upset; it's simply the fact that you are black. That's what makes a racist see red! It's not your denomination or your professional designation, but just your pigmentation.

But if you forget who you are, then you really do start thinking you are better than other black people. You start looking at "them" as beneath you. And some of us will believe it when we're told, "You're different from the other black people. You're a credit to your race." You start thinking and acting like you're superior, and that's thinking and acting like you "is" what you "ain't." The tragedy of it is that sometimes that's learned behavior from our elders. Sometimes the elders, not unlike Mordecai, have given us bad advice. They were worried about our being accepted. They were concerned about our not being liked. They wanted us to talk like white folks talk, to behave like white folks behave. They wanted us to sing like white folks sing. They wanted us to worship like white folks worship. Sometimes the elders have given us bad advice. They have asked us to forget who we are and take on a training program that teaches us that we "is" what we "ain't."

Sometimes the elders have been more concerned about assimilation than they were about liberation. Sometimes they've been more concerned about our going along with slavery than they have been with our getting out of slavery. Sometimes they put so much emphasis on our acculturation that we have lost in the process our soul's salvation. When you're trying to pretend that you "is" what you "ain't," that means that you can't offer to God who you are for God to start working with you where you are. In other words, you can't even be honest with God.

Behavior Determined by Other's Expectations

But when you look at Esther's reply to Mordecai (4:11), telling him how she really couldn't do anything in her Babylonian finery and Babylonian fashions, the third issue of the text is established: She was letting her behavior be determined by the enemy's expectations. When you forget who you are, you start letting your behavior be determined by the enemy's expectations. How you act is based upon what they think. And that sickness is perpetuated, because through assimilation and acculturation, you now think just like they think.

Let me give you an example of how assimilation and acculturation work. Do you ever want to say "amen" but hold back because somebody might not understand? I told you that I'm in a predominantly white denomination. We go somewhere, I preach my heart out, a member comes up to me and grabs my arm and says, "I almost said amen." I say, "Well, why didn't you?" "Well, there were some white people here, and they expect better of me than that."

Have you ever wanted to holler, but you didn't want anybody to look at you? Were you ever more concerned about what somebody else thought than about what you were feeling? Have you ever wanted to say "Thank you, Jesus"? Have you ever wanted to praise God, but you had to cool it because of the role you've been playing, the front you've had to keep up, the position you've attained, and the expectations that went along with that position? If you have, then you can better understand where Esther is in chapter 4, verse 11. I told you she had some serious problems. She couldn't even be for real because she had forgotten who she was. She was letting her behavior be determined by the enemy's expectations. She couldn't act, even though her heart told her that she ought to act, because of what the king might think if she were to break protocol.

Well, it was then that Mordecai saw up close what a magnificent monster he had created with his bad advice that had caused spiritual compromise and cancer of the soul. So he sent back those powerful words that we all know from verses 12 through 14 (GNB). When Mordecai received Esther's message, he sent her this warning: "Don't imagine that you are safer than any other Jew just because you are in the royal palace." Don't you know some of us still think that way?

Let me update Mordecai's message for you. Don't imagine that you are safer than the rest of us just because you are on the city council, or you are in the mayor's chair, or you are in the halls of Congress, or you've got the key to the executive vice president's washroom, or you're at the university. Don't you think that you're any safer than the rest of us because of where you are today.

Many times, thank God, the elders, seeing us substitute acculturation for education, have called us to remembrance and to repentance. My mother and my father pushed me to go to school to get all the education I could, but they kept warning me, "Don't you become no educated fool." You don't let go of what you got in the church house because of what you might get in the school house, the big house, or the White House. Mordecai saw what a mess his first advice had created, so he sent back a warning, "If you keep quiet at a time like this, help will come from heaven to the Jews and they will be saved, but you will die . . . (4:14, GNB).

You see, when you forget who you are, that means that you forget where you came from. When you forget where you came from, that means you have omitted the God factor, the things you learned back in Sunday school. You forget who it was that brought you and who it was that with his precious blood bought you. When you forget who you are, you forget about whose you are. You forget how much you need the Lord. You forget all of those old songs, the ones we used to sing that carried us through the darkest nights, the songs that sustained us when we didn't have half as much as we've got now. Songs like "I Will Trust in the Lord"; songs like "I Love the Lord, He Heard My Cry" — we forget all about those kinds of songs. Don't you know that some of us even join churches where they don't sing those songs anymore. We go to a "Word church."

Because we want our children to have a better Babylonian education, we send them to private schools, where they can get away from all of that old-timey stuff. We forget about God, who was our help in ages past. We forget about God, who is our hope for years to come. We forget about God, who is our shelter from the stormy blast. We forget about our bread in a starving land. We forget about our rock in a weary land. We forget about who it was who made us, and we start thinking of ourselves as self-made.

Sometimes God has to send a Mordecai to remind us that our help still comes from heaven, and that instead of calling on our new-found status, we ought to start falling on our knees and calling on the Lord.

And Esther said, "You're right." We don't need protocol; we need prayer. "Y'all pray for me." That's the learning we know. "My girls and I are going to pray. And if I perish, I perish." I don't know about you, but I don't need pretense; I need prayer. One of the reasons this sermon means so much to me is because a lot of preachers you will hear will preach a gospel that says, "Y'all have sinned and come short of the glory of God." But the Word says, "All have sinned."

I know how this text hits home for me because I used to be just like Esther. I used to let my behavior be determined by the white world's expectations. I used to be afraid or ashamed of who I was and of whose I was. Jim Forbes, pastor of Riverside Church,[19] writes about this predicament in his book *The Holy Spirit in Preaching*. Jim said that he had some problems with his upbringing in the United Holy Church of America and what he learned at Virginia Union and Union Theological Seminaries. See, they taught us at white schools and at many black schools founded by white missionaries that you had to be self-contained and self-controlled. Some members of my congregation say, "Reverend, why do you holler? We have an excellent P.A. system. If one is truly educated, one does not get emotional." And there I was, with two degrees from Howard and another degree from the University of Chicago Divinity School. I was pastoring a United Church of Christ church in a predominantly white denomination, and my white colleagues could not understand. Like Jim, I couldn't reconcile my past with my present. And some of you have been there, too. Some of "y'all" are still there. I used to be afraid to say amen. I used to be afraid to move when the music got good. I used to be too embarrassed to cry if I felt like crying, to shout if the Spirit said shout. I was letting what the enemy thought determine how I would behave.

Jim said he kept on hearing Carlyle Marney[20] say, "Jim, no person ever amounts to much until he or she learns to bless his or her own origins." And I found out that I had to start blessing my origins. So one night a brother heard me talking about Virginia. He said, "Where do your parents come from?" My dad isn't from the city. My mom's from Surrey County. My daddy's from Caroline County. Those are my origins. And I bless God for those origins. And I found out in blessing my own origins, that it ain't about what

other folk think about me, and it ain't about what other folk
expect of me. It's all about what the Lord has done for me. I
don't need the enemy. I don't need no image. I don't need no
broadcloth. I don't need no pedigree. I do need somebody to
tell me every now and then, "Fight on! Preach on! Hold on!
Run on!"

Study Questions

1. In order for the Hebrew girl Hadassah to become
Queen Esther, she experienced "assimilation" and "acculturation." Explain how African Americans have undergone a
similar change.

2. Why does the Surinamese chief's question to the two
researchers, "Why do you wear the clothes of the enemy"
stir such intense emotions?

3. How would you answer the chief's question?

4. The two researchers told the chief that they were still
fighting their war with the white devil. Assuming that you
agree with them, what examples would you give of this ongoing fight?

5. Many people criticize Hispanics who do not learn the
English language and who would prefer that all official
transactions be bilingual. Are they refusing to become assimilated? Should the rest of society learn to speak Spanish?

6. Do people living in a cultural plurality need to assimilate? In what ways? In what ways can people maintain their
own ethnic identities?

7. Do you believe that ethnic and cultural identities are
God-given? Can you base your belief, pro or con, in Scrip-

ture? How do you view the statement that persons cannot offer themselves to God or even be honest with God when pretending that they "is" what they "ain't?"

8. How do we reconcile ourselves with the sins of our elders? Remember Mordecai's bad advice to Hadassah. How can we make our peace with our elders, forgiving some of the bad advice concerning assimilation that they handed down to us?

9. How can we help ourselves and others break free from feelings of superiority or inferiority based upon the degree to which we or they have or have not become assimilated? Do we still poke fun at "country" folks who lack the polish of the more acculturated? Do we recognize our behaviors that indicate feelings of superiority toward others?

10. Give a testimony about how you came to be and to love yourself. Tell how you overcame the need for others' approval, particularly the approval of the majority culture. Include examples of your unique ethnicity that you maintain as part of your identity and freedom.

Full of the Holy Spirit

Acts 6:8-15; 7:54-80; 8:1

John Ansbro's book about Martin Luther King[1] talks about Dr. King's education and the influence of the school at Boston on his life;[2] it talks about his education at Morehouse and Dr. Benjamin Mays' influence on him;[3] it talks about his seminary education at Crozer Theological Seminary. But it does not talk about the fact that Martin Luther King was a minister of the gospel, a Baptist minister born and bred in the church. Nor is there one word in all of that learned treatise about the fact that Martin Luther King was a man full of the Holy Spirit.

The Lord blessed my life in recent years by allowing me to team up with a gentleman by the name of Dr. John Kinney. Dr. Kinney is the dean of the School of Theology at Virginia Union University. Twice a year for two years we were teamed up in Harrisburg and Pittsburgh in teaching and preaching revivals. One of the many things that Dr. Kinney taught me was the importance of what he calls "sidewalk theology." This Ph.D. student of King and Cone[4] explained that after a lecture, a presentation, or a sermon, when he was away from the podium, the auditorium, the sanctuary, and the pulpit, various preachers in city-wide meetings or conferees at conferences would stop him on the sidewalk and ask him questions that they could not ask on the inside. They would engage him in conversation that they felt was a little rough or too touchy for the lecture hall. It was in those conversations that he said he found himself engaged in doing "sidewalk theology."

Heavy conversations took place on the sidewalk, life-and-death conversations that got to the root of what people believe they have been taught and mistaught. Dr. Kinney taught me that some of the most important teaching goes on right there on the sidewalk, and he influenced me to listen to those questions and concerns that come up away from a classroom, away from a lecture, away from an institute, because some of those questions are far more crucial in terms of where people really are and in terms of what it is that is eating at them.

I thank God for that lesson from Dr. Kinney, because I have learned to listen with a different ear when people engage me in those conversations. I have also come up with a first cousin for Dr. Kinney's sidewalk theology; it's called cafeteria theology.

Cafeteria Theology

While walking through the cafeteria before service at Olivet Baptist Church in Memphis, where I participate in a teaching and preaching revival every year, I have had questions asked of me that folks were afraid to ask me in the sanctuary. I found myself doing cafeteria theology.

Somebody wanted to know about marrying a man who did not believe in the church that Jesus founded, that he shed his blood for, and that he is coming back for. Somebody asked me, as a pastor, "Would you marry somebody who does not go to church and believe in church while you are trying to raise your child in the church? Would you marry somebody who does not believe in what you stand for? And, Reverend, would you perform the ceremony?" These are cafeteria questions.

And somebody who didn't understand how a preacher and jazz music went into the same paragraph was asking me about Wynton Marsalis and jazz music.[5] Somebody wanted to know about homosexuality because he had some good friends who were homosexuals, some family members who were homosexuals, and because he himself was a homosexual. He did not understand why God made him that way and how the church could condemn him for being the way

God made him. These are cafeteria questions—crucial questions that reflect where people are and what it is that is really eating at them.

I learned to listen with a different ear when people began to engage in these kinds of conversations, and it was in a cafeteria theology session that I heard another question that hits right where many of us live. I had been preaching at Olivet on the anointing of the Holy Spirit, about what happens when God sends the anointing, how the anointing makes the difference, breaks yokes, heals splits, restores and makes us whole. I had been preaching on how the Holy Spirit makes us remember, how he makes us feel and do good, and how he restores us to the way we were when God first created us. I had been preaching about the Holy Spirit, and one of the members of Olivet stopped me and said, "Reverend Wright, what does it mean to be full of the Holy Spirit?"

Memphis is the headquarters of the Church of God in Christ, and this member of Olivet said, "I have friends and co-workers who are Pentecostals, and they tell me that those of us who are in the Baptist Church or the A.M.E. church[6], or any other church besides their church ain't saved. In fact, when Pastor Whalum told us to invite someone to the revival, I asked that Pentecostal friend of mine. She asked me who was preaching, and I told her Reverend Lawson, Reverend Adams, and you, and she said, 'Ain't none of y'all saved.' When I told my friend about you preaching on the Holy Spirit, she said that any church that had women preachers and women deacons didn't know anything about the Holy Spirit. She told me that I ought to watch Fred Price and that only the ministers from her church were Spirit-filled, or full of the Holy Spirit. So I need to know, Reverend Wright, what does it mean to be full of the Holy Spirit?"

The woman said, "Does it mean that you got to speak in tongues? I got one co-worker who starts praying in tongues even over the food we eat at lunch." She said, "I'm sitting over here praying, 'God, make us truly grateful for the food we are about to receive for the nourishment of our bodies,' and she's sitting on the other side speaking in tongues. I asked her what she was saying, and she said she doesn't know what she's saying. Now I don't know what she's saying, she don't know what she's saying, and I got the feeling God don't know what she's saying. So I asked her why she does that. And she said she was full of the Holy Spirit. Is that what it means to be full of the Holy Spirit? Or does it mean you don't sin no more?"

The woman continued, "One of my children has gone over to the Pentecostal church because that is where her 'sweet thing' belongs. And now she comes back and tells me that she is living free from sin because she is full of the Holy Spirit. Now, I know what my child is doing. I overhear the phone calls; I do check the love letters she leaves lying around. And I'm already paying for a grandbaby that don't have two parents. I know my child. She's saved from the top of her head to the tip of her navel. And when I asked her about that, she said that the Lord gonna take care of that, too, because she's full of the Holy Spirit. Well, I know that my child is lying, but when you are full of the Holy Spirit, does it really mean you don't sin no more? What does it mean to be full of the Holy Spirit?"

This was a crucial question in terms of where this member of Olivet really was and what it was that was really eating at her. Plus, I learned something else apart from what Dr. Kinney had already taught me about sidewalk or cafeteria theology: Sometimes when a person is stuck on a crucial question, there is a blockage in hearing what the man, woman, or Word of God is saying until that question is addressed. Maybe the question is not answered, but it at least must be addressed.

Sometimes, therefore, it is necessary to address a question to help a person get unstuck so that he or she can move on to hear what God has to say. You remember the woman at the well, don't you?[7] The Lord wanted her to know that she counted and that he cared for her and came for her and that he had just what she needed. But before she could hear any of that, Jesus had to get her unstuck by addressing her questions. "You, a Jew, talking to me, a Samaritan? Where are we supposed to worship? My people say it's right here; your people say it's down in Jerusalem." She was stuck. What she was talking about had nothing to do with what the Lord wanted her to hear, but she couldn't receive what the Lord had to give because she was stuck on the issue of place. Jesus was talking about salvation, and she was stuck on the issue of location. So Jesus addressed her question in order to help her move on past it to hear what he had to say. It is sometimes necessary to address a question to help a person get unstuck.

Second, I learned that many times a crucial question for one person is a nagging question for somebody else. The one for whom it is a nagging question has just never raised it. He or she just hangs around, listening, and hoping to get an answer while I talk with someone else. Take, for instance, the homosexual question that day in the cafeteria. When the question was raised and I started to answer, I felt like Jesus in Matthew 5, up on the mountain when the multitude came to him. As I began to address the question, folks came from everywhere to hear the answer although only one person had raised the question. Or, when the Olivet member asked me in the cafeteria about being full of the Holy Spirit, six people who were sitting at the table stopped eating some "sho' nuff" down-home Tennessee cooking to hear what I was going to say. They didn't raise the question; only one person did.

So, having learned these two additional things, let me share with you my answer to the member from Olivet in order that somebody might get unstuck and be blessed. I told this member of Olivet, "I don't know what your co-worker means when she says 'full of the Holy Spirit.' And I don't know what your child means when your child says 'full of the Holy Spirit.' I do know what Fred Price teaches, and I also know what the Pentecostal church teaches, but since the Pentecostals have only been around for 100 years, and since Fred Price hasn't been around for a good 55 years yet, let's go back to the Word of God, because the Word of God

has been around for at least a couple of thousand years, and
the Spirit of God has been around empowering humankind
for at least another 5,000 years. So let us see what the Word
of God has to say about being full of the Holy Spirit."

Now, there were many places that we could have looked to
get some biblical insights into this crucial question. We
could have looked at Moses, the man who was called a friend
of God, the only one who talked to God face-to-face.[8] Surely
Moses was a man who was full of the Holy Spirit. We could
have looked at David, who was called a man after God's own
heart, the one who wrote, "Create in me a clean heart, O
God, and renew a right spirit within me. Cast me not away
from thy presence; and take not thy holy spirit from me."[9]
Surely David was a man who was full of the Holy Spirit.

We could have looked at Deborah, the wife of Lappidoth,
the woman who was a prophetess and who served as a judge
in Israel for forty years, twice as long as Samson.[10] Deborah
led ten thousand men into battle against Sisera, and mas-
terminded the victory at Mount Tabor. Surely Deborah was
a woman who was full of the Holy Spirit.

We could have looked at Ruth, the wife of Chilion and
daughter-in-law of Naomi. Ruth, the woman from Moab,
who when offered a chance to go back to her people, under
the unction of the Holy Spirit uttered those immortal
words: "Entreat me not to leave thee, or to return from following after thee: for whither thou goest I will go; and
where thou lodgest, I will lodge: thy people shall be my
people, and thy God my God."[11] Surely Ruth was a woman
who was full of the Holy Spirit.

We could have looked at Elijah, the preacher who confronted Ahab and Jezebel in all of their wickedness; the
preacher, who with the hand of the Lord upon him, outran
Ahab's chariot all the way from Mount Carmel to Jezreel;[12]
the preacher who dueled four hundred and fifty prophets of
Baal in a praying match, and his prayers were so powerful
that God rained down fire from heaven;[13] the preacher who
had a chariot from heaven sent to chauffeur him back to
glory.[14] Surely Elijah was a man full of the Holy Spirit.

We could have looked at Isaiah, the one who in the year that King Uzziah died saw also the Lord sitting high and lifted up on a throne.[15] Isaiah was the prophet who wrote some 734 years before the event, "For unto us a child is born, unto us a son is given: and the government shall be upon his shoulder: and his name shall be called Wonderful, Counselor, The mighty God, The everlasting Father, The Prince of Peace."[16] Surely Isaiah was full of the Holy Spirit. He wrote: "Every valley shall be exalted, and every mountain and hill shall be made low: the crooked shall be made straight, and the rough places plain: and the glory of the LORD shall be revealed, and all flesh shall see it together: for the mouth of the LORD has spoken it."[17]

Surely Isaiah was full of the Holy Spirit when he wrote, "He was wounded for our transgressions, he was bruised for our iniquities: the chastisement of our peace was upon him; and with his stripes we are healed."[18] And again, was it not under the unction of the Holy Spirit that Isaiah declared, "Hast thou not known? Hast thou not heard, that the everlasting God, the LORD, the Creator of the ends of the earth, fainteth not, neither is weary? . . . He giveth power to the faint; and to them that have no might he increaseth strength. Even the youths shall faint and be weary, and the young men shall utterly fall: but they that wait upon the LORD shall renew their strength; they shall mount up with wings as eagles; they shall run, and not be weary; and they shall walk, and not faint."[19] Surely Isaiah was a man who was full of the Holy Spirit.

There are many places that we could have looked to get some biblical insights into what it means to be full of the Holy Spirit, but I asked her to look with me at the sixth and seventh chapters of the book of The Acts of the Apostles. Here in Acts 6 is where the apostles tell the believers to choose seven from their ranks who are known to be full of the Holy Spirit. And we started here in Acts 6 to get some biblical insight into what being full of the Holy Spirit really means. The first textual clue we saw was the issue of inspiration. That's when God breathes his breath upon you. It is

written that Stephen was a man who was richly blessed by
God and full of power. When you are full of the Holy Spirit,
you are richly blessed by God and full of power.

Spirit-filled Christians Have Inspiration That Unleashes Power

Now, we are all blessed by God. We are blessed to have
eyes to see, legs to walk, voices to talk, food to eat, clothes
to wear, a blood family, a church family, grace that is still
sufficient, a Christ who cares, and somebody right now
making intercession on our behalf. We are blessed to have a
God who is able to do exceedingly, abundantly above all
that we have thought, hoped, or asked. We are blessed to
have a God who will supply our every need. We are blessed
by God.

But when you are full of the Holy Spirit, you are richly
blessed. You have more than you know what to do with.
Your cup just runs over. And you are full of power – not your
power, but God's power. You have power to love your enemies, even when they are stoning you, like Stephen who was
stoned. You have power to love.

You know, Dr. Samuel Proctor, one of my teachers and
my mentor in the Proctor Program,[20] said, "I don't have one
enemy on the whole earth. There is not a person living or
breathing who is my enemy. I love everybody." Now I'm sitting there. I've known Dr. Proctor since I was a freshman at
Virginia Union back in 1959. And I've just met a woman at
the Black Theology Project who was from Abyssinian
Church[21] and who couldn't stand Dr. Proctor. Even my
mother knew, so I called my mother to find out what in the
world had happened in this lady's life to make her hate Dr.
Proctor the way she did. My mama said, "Son, it goes way
back to after Adam Clayton Powell died, and you wouldn't
understand."

And I knew this woman didn't like him, so I said to Dr.
Proctor, "You have no enemies on the face of the earth." And
he said, "No, not one." I said, "What about Dr. _____?" He
said, "She's not my enemy. She's just one of my many confused friends."

The Holy Spirit gives you power to love your "confused friends" even when they are stoning you the way they stoned Stephen. You have power to bless those who curse you and to pray for those who despitefully use you. You have power to do things you never dreamed about doing because you are not doing them under your power, but under his power. You have power to smile when your heart is heavy, to laugh when you feel like crying, to work when you don't feel like working, and to pray when you sometimes don't feel like praying. You have power because what you have in you is inspiration (Latin *inspirare*, literally, "to breathe into," from *in* + *spirare*, "to breathe"), God's Spirit breathing into your spirit. You have God's Spirit working on you, in you, through you, and for you. This inspiration (breathed-in spirit) gives you power to get up and do while all of the others around you are sitting around talking about what can't be done.

We have power to educate our own children about the history and heritage of Africa, a subject that the public school systems won't teach them. We have power to teach our own African American people about the intangible things that money can never buy, and we have power to do it without waiting for somebody else to do it. We have power to take our own communities back from the junkies and the drug dealers. Do you want to know what being full of the Holy Spirit means? It means power to run drugs and drug dealers right on back underneath the rock that they crawled out from under.

Let me ask you something: How is it that Muslims can run the dealers out of their community and the Christians sit around helpless but say that they follow a man who's got all power in his hands? A quick footnote: Don't you let anybody trick you into thinking Minister Louis Farrakhan[22] is your enemy. He ain't the enemy. Any African man who can clean folks up, get them off of dope, get them in school, get them reading instead of rapping, get them building each other up, is not the enemy. He isn't the enemy. The enemy is the one bringing the drugs into your country, into your community, your block, and your house. Some folks are tricky.

They will try to make you choose between Malcolm and Martin. Don't you let them. No, no. If you have been helped by both, say "hallelujah!" for both of them.

And they are not going to make me choose between Minister Jackson and Minister Farrakhan. When Jesse is right, he's my friend; when Louis is right, he's my friend. When Jesse is wrong, he is still my friend; when Louis is wrong, he is still my friend. You don't give up a friendship because you have a disagreement. That ain't no friend! Don't let them make you choose.

And let me tell you something: I have power. And I follow a man who has all power, and there's nothing any Muslim can do that I can't do. Holy Ghost power will help you take your community back from drug dealers. That's what being full of the Holy Spirit means.

Being full of the Holy Spirit means being filled with God's breath—inspiration. You've got power to take over and build a community for your own grandchildren to grow up in and to be what God created them to be. When you are full of the Holy Spirit, you are richly blessed by God. That's what Isaiah was saying: "He gives power to the faint, and strengthens the powerless" (Isaiah 40:29, NRSV).

Long before there were any doctrinal definitions of different denominations and cute little faith formulas about the Holy Spirit, there were Africans who were teaching us by examples (not unlike Stephen and King) what it meant to have this kind of power. They were like that cute little toy that my grandson has. Have you ever seen the toy the kids play with that comes back up when you knock it down? No matter how hard you hit it, it comes back up. You can hit it with your fist, and it comes back up. You can take a stick and hit it, and it will still come back up. Well, every time those Africans were hit, they came back up. I don't care how hard they were hit, they came back up. They were hit with slavery and segregation; they came back up. They were hit with racism and degradation; they came back up. One little boy who had that kind of toy told his daddy, "I know why you can't knock it down, Daddy." "Why?" asked his father. "Cause it's got another little man on the inside that's standing up."

Africans taught us by their lives that God will give you an inner strength that keeps you upright like that "little man" inside the toy. God will give you power to stand up on the inside, and you learn that once you stand up on the inside, nothing and nobody can knock you down on the outside.

The Spirit-filled Christian Has Dedication

The next clue in this text to what being full of the Holy Spirit means is the issue of dedication: doing great things for the purpose of pointing to God. This text says that Stephen performed miracles and wonders among the people. Miracles and wonders are never just isolated phenomena performed to baffle the human mind. No, miracles and wonders were always given to point those who saw them to the experience of God. I thank one of the preachers from Houston for showing this to our church. Reverend A. Lewis Patterson[23] said a lot of us become confused when we look at the miracle, as if it were the central thing. The miracles aren't anything but signs pointing to God. Here's the difference. When you get hungry this evening and go down the street and see the golden arches of McDonald's, that's just the sign. You don't stop and sit on the sign and say, "Well, I'm eating now. I'm at McDonald's."

On the way home from Texas to Chicago, we saw a sign that said "Highway 10." We were coming out of New Orleans, and it said "Beaumont." I said, "Beaumont? Where is that?" Someone said, "It's in Texas." I said, "But we are in New Orleans." The sign was only pointing that way. When you see a sign it doesn't mean that you've gotten there yet. A lot of us get confused with doing great things. We want to point to ourselves. Stephen wasn't doing things to point to himself. He was dedicated, calling people to point them to God, pointing to something much higher and much more important than himself.

We've got folks right now doing great things that point to God—nothing spectacular, no, but very great things such as spending time shaping the lives of young black boys and girls, giving them some positive role models to counter all of the junk they see on television. Those are great things that

point to God. Taking the time to talk to a young boy about
the Lord because his own daddy is too busy or too absent—
that's a great thing that points to God. Dedication is the
doing of great things that point to God.

Spirit-filled Christians Experience Confrontation

Verse 9 is a whole sermon by itself. It says that being full
of the Holy Spirit does not free you from opposition. You
will be opposed, even by some in the church. In verse 9 arguing takes place in the church. Dr. King faced opposition in
both the local and the national church, as well as in various
meetings and within the civil rights movement. A whole lot
of preachers opposed what King stood for while he was
alive, and some still do years after his death.

Opposition takes place in verse 9, and trickery in verses
10 and 11. In verse 12 they stir up a mess, and in verse 13
they lie about Stephen. Satan is the father of lies, according
to the Bible,[24] so that means that Satan was active in the
church. Being full of the Holy Spirit means that you will be
opposed by Satan in the same way that black folks have
been opposed by Satan since he was brought into the church
by slave-trading hypocrites. Being opposed by Satan means
confrontation. We have been confronted by the evils of miseducation and false definition of who we were and where we
came from. We have been confronted by separate schools
and bath facilities, separate classrooms and washrooms. We
have been confronted by inferior equipment and inferior estimates of our self-worth. And we have been confronted by
racist theology and racist sociology, racist anthropology
and racist psychology. Satan has confronted us every step
of the way. Being full of the Holy Spirit means being opposed by Satan, the father of lies.

Satan will be brought into the church now like he was
brought into the church then, but verses 10 and 15 of chapter 6 and all of chapter 7 say something else. They teach us
that in addition to inspiration, dedication, and confrontation, being full of the Holy Spirit also means transformation.

Spirit-filled Christians Are Transformed People

God changes you. God changes the way you look, in spite of opposition, in spite of being opposed, lied on, lied to, and lied about. Stephen just looked different. He experienced transformation. Have you ever met somebody who was so changed on the inside that he or she looked different on the outside? That's why I don't understand a lot of folks in churches I visit around this country. They love the Lord, but they look like everybody else. If the Lord has done something for you, it ought to show on your face. It ought to change the way you look. In verse 10 the Word says the Spirit made Stephen talk tough, because the Spirit also changes the way you talk. He talked so tough that his enemies or his "confused friends" did not know how to act. All of chapter 7, from verse 2 to verse 53 shows Stephen talking about the Lord. When is the last time you were in church and did not talk about anything but the Lord? Not about gossip or what the choirs were singing or who your favorite soloist was; not about robes or dinners, but about the Lord. That's what Stephen did. Being full of the Holy Spirit changes the way you look and the way you talk.

It also changes what you see. Look at verse 55, chapter 7. Stephen, full of the Holy Spirit, looked up to heaven and saw God's glory and Jesus sitting at God's right hand. When you look up, it changes what you see. With enemies all around you, look up. With failure all around you, look up. With disappointment all around you, look up. With our community needing some rejuvenation, look up. With our young people needing hope instead of dope, look up. With our families needing God, look up. With our souls needing a Savior, look up. When you look up, it changes you. It changes what you see. Transformation starts taking place. Problems get transformed into possibilities when you look up. Calamities get transformed into opportunities when you look up. Negatives get transformed into positives when you look up. Defeat is transformed into victory when you look up. Stumbling blocks get transformed into stepping stones when you look up. Crucifixions get transformed into resurrections when you look up.

That old saying "I just can't . . ." gets transformed into "I
can do all things through [Christ] who strengthens me"[25]
when you look up. And that saying you hear in our community, "We can't do nothing about that problem," gets transformed into "If God is for us, who is against us"[26] when you
look up. When you look up, what you see is changed.

Verse 60 says being full of the Holy Spirit changes how
you react to the hatred. Even while the wrong was being
done to Stephen, he asked God to forgive the wrong doers.
Being full of the Holy Spirit does not stop folks from hating
you, but it does change how you react to that hatred. Bigoted folks are still bigoted folks. The ones you left Friday
afternoon back at your job will be waiting for you on Monday morning, but you can get up tomorrow praising God
anyhow, because bigoted folks didn't make the day; God
made the day. They didn't make you; God made you. They
didn't die for you; the Lord died for you. They are not worthy to be praised, but the Lord is worthy to be praised. How
you react to hatred gets changed. Transformation takes
place.

Spirit-filled Christians Anticipate God's Intervention

But then there is one more thing this text teaches me: Being filled with the Holy Spirit means anticipation. God
says, "Receive my spirit." You see, you get up every day expecting God to do something great – anticipation. You get
up every morning expecting God to supply you with fresh
grace – anticipation. You're resting as if God will do what he
has already done. Like my grandmama used to say, "He's
already done what he said he would do," so you just get up
expecting more of the same. Anticipation is knowing that
God is acting on the problem even though that action is not
visible.

The best example I've seen of this happened last summer
in the city of Chicago. A girl and her daddy were enjoying a
peaceful afternoon on Lake Michigan. He had been com-
plaining about everything always being mother and daughter or father and son, so he took his only daughter out on
Lake Michigan for an afternoon of sailing. Tragically, water

came pouring through a hole in the bottom of the boat and the boat was at the bottom of Lake Michigan within two minutes. Now he could swim, but she couldn't. The problem was that he had a bad heart and had had aortic valve surgery. With his weak heart, he couldn't swim the quarter of a mile back to the beach, and pull her all at the same time. So he said, "Baby, do you remember how I taught you to float?" And she said, "Yes." He said, "Well, you turn on your back and float."

She turned on her back and started floating. He said, "Daddy is going to get help and I'm coming back for you." And he swam that quarter of a mile onto the beach at Fifty-fifth Street. Only when he got there, there were no boats. So he thumbed a ride down to the Navy pier, down around Twelfth Street. At the navy pier he got on a Coast Guard boat, and by the time they got back to Fifty-fifth Street, over an hour had elapsed, and there was no sign of his daughter. The boat started making wider and wider circles, and the day started coming to an end.

The Coast Guard wanted to stop, but the man kept making them go wider and wider, until they had gone out four miles into Lake Michigan. He said as the sun was setting, "Can we take one more sweep?" They said, "Yes." But they knew it was in vain (so they thought). When they took that last sweep, they saw a little red dress bobbing about 400 yards out on the water. Knowing that she was dead, they determined to hold him in the boat because he wanted to jump back in the water and swim to his daughter. They restrained him and said, "We're going out there, sir." They opened it up and went toward his daughter. Instead of finding her dead as they had assumed she would be, when they got about 20 yards from her, they found her floating on the water and singing, "Be not dismayed, whate'er betide, God will take care of you."[27]

They asked her, "Baby, how could you last this long?" "It was easy," she said. "My daddy said he was coming back for me, and my daddy never breaks his promises."

We have a father who is coming back for us. You anticipate. God will take care of you. My Father has said he is coming back, and God has never broken his promise. Think back to when King was killed. Think back. God will take care of you. Think back when they murdered King. It looked like it was all over—hopeless and helpless—but God will take care of you. Twenty-one years later what has God done? God gave us black mayors in Chicago, Birmingham, Atlanta, New York; a black governor in Virginia; a Ron McNair out of Texas, along with a Barbara Jordan and Mickey Leland. God will take care of you. "No matter what may be the test, God will take care of you. Lean, weary one, upon his breast. God will take care of you."[28]

Study Questions

1. Using the concept of "cafeteria theology," coin a term that fits your situation for those informal and unplanned encounters that you have experienced which allowed you to share the crucial and nagging questions of others. Use this sermon's definitions of "crucial" and "nagging" in formulating your response.

2. Recall instances where you or someone you know was "stuck" like the woman at the well (John 4) and therefore unable to receive God's Word. How can you, as a friend, parent, family member, teacher, counselor, minister, or just one who prayerfully listens, help people get past those places in their minds and hearts where they are stuck?

3. Before reading this sermon, what was your notion of what it means to be filled with the Holy Spirit? What was your religious training pertaining to this subject?

4. Has this sermon enhanced or changed your idea of what it means to be filled with the Holy Spirit? Please explain.

5. The strict or literal meaning of "inspiration" is "to breathe into." How can you apply this concept of the Spirit's in-filling to your everyday circumstances?

6. Look at Satan's temptation of Jesus in the wilderness (Matthew 4:1-11; Luke 4:1-13). In what ways did these temptations test Jesus' dedication to his Father's will and purpose for his life?

7. Spirit-filled Christians often experience confrontation, yet sometimes Christians overuse this concept, attributing everything that comes against them, from a stubbed toe to a life-threatening disease, to a confrontation with Satan. Using at least one of the textual clue words (inspiration, dedication, transformation, anticipation), explain why Stephen's confrontation was a genuine bout with the devil. (For example, Stephen's confrontation with persons motivated by Satan was in direct response to his _____, as shown in verses _____ of the text.) Do these clue words help you discern a true confrontation from a false one? What other criteria would you use?

8. The "transformed" Christian's life reflects newness. In the African American tradition, the elders said of this experience, "I looked at my hands and they were new. I looked at my feet, and they were, too." What are some Scriptures that speak of the newness of the Spirit-filled life? Share personal experiences of transformation.

9. In Acts 1:8 (KJV), Jesus tells his disciples, "But ye shall receive power, after the Holy Ghost is come upon you: and ye shall be my witnesses. . . ." Give examples of the power of the Holy Ghost in the Bible, in history, in your own life and in the lives of others you know. How does this power distinguish us as unique witnesses?

10. The hopeful anticipation experienced by the little girl who was rescued from the boating accident is a gripping ex-

ample of the Christian's anticipation of all that God will do immediately, in the future, and beyond this life. How can we nurture and keep fresh such a spirit of anticipation within ourselves? Use as a reference Matthew 18:3.

The Audacity to Hope

I Samuel 1:1-18

Several years ago, when I was in Richmond, Virginia, at the Fifth Street Baptist Church, the Lord fixed it so that I was there at the same time that the convocation was being held at Virginia Union University School of Theology. I said the Lord fixed it because I was able to conduct a revival at the church in the evenings and to attend the convocation services during the daytime. It was at those convocation services that my life was blessed like it has never been blessed before, as I sat under the preaching of the eminent pastor of the Tabernacle Baptist Church of Detroit, the Reverend Dr. Frederick G. Sampson.

In one of the sermons he delivered that week, he talked about a painting that I had studied in humanities at this same school when I had been a student there years before. The painting is by a man named Watt. It is a painting that seems at first glance to be a study in contradictions, because what is designated as the title of the painting and what is depicted on the canvas of the painting seem to be in direct opposition to each other. In fact, Dr. Sampson said that when he first saw the painting, he wanted to quarrel with the artist for misnaming it and for playing such a cruel joke on art lovers who had religious sensibilities.

You see, the painting is entitled *Hope*. It shows a woman who is playing a harp sitting on top of the world. Now that by itself would be all right, for what more enviable position could any of us ever hope to be in than being on top of the

world with everything and everybody dancing to our music.
But when you look closer at the painting, when the illusion
of power starts giving way to the reality of pain, the world
on which this woman sits—our world—is one torn by war,
destroyed by hate, decimated by despair, and devastated by
distrust. The world, in fact, is on the very brink of destruction, and Watt depicted that in what he put on the canvas,
thereby contradicting what is evoked by the title *Hope*.

In our world, famine ravishes black and brown citizens
who make up one-half or two-thirds of the globe, while feast-
ing and gluttony are enjoyed by the minority of persons
who inhabit the globe. I don't know if you have ever been on
one of those cruise ships that go to the Caribbean, but you
do know of the hunger that is in such places as Haiti. Each
week when those ships come back into Miami or San Juan,
they dump more food into the Atlantic Ocean or the Caribbean Sea than the hungry citizens in Haiti can find to eat in
a lifetime.

With apartheid in one hemisphere and apathy in the
other hemisphere, and enough nuclear warheads stockpiled
to wipe out all forms of life except for cockroaches, the
world on which the woman is sitting is a world on the very
brink of destruction. It is a world that cares more about
bombs for the enemy than bread for the hungry; a world
that is more concerned about the color of skin than about
the content of character; a world that is more finicky about
the texture of hair or what's on the outside of your head
than it is about the quality of education or what is on the
inside of your head. That is the world on which this woman
is sitting.

We think of being on top of the world as being in heaven.
But when you look closely, all in fact is hell. The harpist is
sitting there in rags. Her clothes are tattered as though she,
herself, had been a victim of Hiroshima or the Sharpeville
Massacre.[1] When you look at her closely, you see a bandage
on her head with blood beginning to seep through. Scars
and cuts are visible on her face, arms, and legs, and the harp
on which she is playing has all but one of its strings torn,
ripped out, dangling down. Even her instrument has been

damaged by what she has been through, and she is more the classic example of quiet despair than anything else, yet the artist dared to entitle this painting *Hope*.

When you look closer at what the artist did on the canvas — the illusion of power giving way to the reality of pain — you may ask, Isn't that just the way it is with so many of us? We give the illusion of being in an enviable position, but when you look closer at our lives, what you begin to find is the reality of a pain sometimes too deep for the tongue to tell. Like the woman in Watt's painting we may appear to be living in heaven, but our existence is actually a quiet hell.

I've seen too many people not to know what I am talking about. Sometimes it's a married couple where the husband has a lady in addition to his wife. The wife smiles and keeps on stepping. Or she goes shopping to buy something with the thought that maybe things can make up for the most important thing missing in her life. Perhaps she pretends she doesn't hear the whispers. She ignores the gossip and remembers that she has the papers on him. And he would rather buy Fort Knox than file for divorce from her because of what she would make him pay. That's a living hell.

Or maybe it's a married couple where the wife has discovered that somebody cares for her as a person and not just as the cook, the maid, the jitney service, and the call girl service all wrapped into one. And now there is the scandal of what the folks might say and what the children might think. She has all of that to think about. A living hell.

Maybe it's a divorced person whose dreams have been blown to bits. The family has been broken up beyond repair, and the lives of parents and children have somehow slipped right through their fingers. They no longer have any control. If she is a divorced woman, the dudes automatically assume she must be missing a man, and that is exactly how they approach her: "Hey baby, let me rap with you." A living hell. If he is a divorced male, a single black man with a j-o-b, and in the church, you can imagine how they come at him. A living hell.

College kids and high school kids wear designer labels, engage in all the sex they want, and smoke all the reefers[2]

they can get, exhibiting the trappings of having it all together on the outside, but they're empty, shallow, hurting,
lonely, and afraid on the inside. A living hell. A lot of things
that look good on the outside don't feel good on the inside.

Martin Luther King had what looked good on the outside. He had it all: a Ph.D. from Boston University, the pastorate of a prestigious church in one of the nation's leading
southern cities, national recognition and international
fame, a Nobel Peace Prize, and a voice known in every home
in the country. It looked good on the outside. But he had to
contend with jealousy among his lieutenants; hounding by
Hoover, along with the FBI wiretappings; threats on his life
and bomb scares for his family; preachers trying to steal his
church and preachers trying to steal his thunder. There was
public tension between his movement and those the media
called the militants. He was unwelcome in Chicago, disre-
spected by Daley, jerked around by J.H. Jackson, and opposed by some preachers, and misunderstood by impatient
young blacks who were tired of waiting and disenchanted
with nonviolence.[3] What looked good on the outside was a
living hell for King on the inside.

What looks like being in heaven is often existence in a
quiet hell. And this is exactly where Hannah is in the first
chapter of 1 Samuel.

Hannah was top dog in a three-way relationship that con-
sisted of herself, Elkanah, and Peninnah. Elkanah loved her
more than he loved his other wife and her children. He told
her he loved her (a lot of us husbands never do that), and he
showed her he loved her (and many husbands still don't do
that). In fact, it was her husband's attention and his affec-
tion for her that caused Peninnah to stay so consistently on
Hannah's case. Jealousy will get a hold of you, and you
won't be able to let it go, because it won't let you go. Peninnah stayed on Hannah like white on rice: "Miss Fine. First
Lady. Miss Grand. Well, you got the paycheck, but these
children show you what I got. I didn't have them by myself."

At first glance Hannah's position was enviable. She had
all of the rights and none of the responsibilities: no diapers
to change, no noses to wipe, no beds to sit up next to late at
night when there were fevers, no clothes to keep clean, no

cuts and bruises to bandage, no medicine to force down, no infants' mouths draining you of milk, no stretch marks. Hannah had it all! Top dog! She had all of the rights and none of the responsibilities. Her man loved her; everybody knew that. He loved her more than anything or anybody. That's why Peninnah couldn't stand her. Except for this second wife thing, Hannah was sitting on top of the world, until you look closer. When you look closer, what looked like being in heaven was actually living in hell. What looked like power was, in reality, pain.

Hannah had to contend with the pain of a bitter woman. Verse 7 says Peninnah's mouth was nonstop. Year after year this went on every time they traveled to Shiloh for what should have been a happy occasion. Every time they went there Peninnah saw to it that Hannah lived in pure hell. Motor mouth.

Hannah not only had the pain of this bitter woman to contend with, but she had the additional pain of a barren womb. In biblical days a woman with a barren womb was a study of deep pathos and distress. (Remember the story of Elizabeth and her husband in Luke 1?) Hannah's world was flawed. Her garments of respectability were tattered and torn, and her heart was bruised and bleeding because of the constant attacks of a jealous woman. The scars and scratches on her psyche were almost visible in this passage as she cried and refused to eat anything. Like the woman in Watt's painting, Hannah, who seemed to live in heaven was actually existing in a quiet hell.

Existence in a Quiet Hell

Let's return to something Dr. Sampson said. He said that at first he wanted to argue with the artist for calling that picture *Hope*. Well, I was sitting there listening to him, and the Lord fixed it for me because I was living in a quiet hell. It was many years ago, and I was the parent of a fifteen-year-old daughter who was in love, love, love, endless love. The boy was twenty years old, too old for her, but he wouldn't leave her alone. Sampson was preaching about hope, and all I had on my mind was murder.

You think about what you are going through. I'm telling

you about what I was going through while he talked about hope. He said that the artist had created a problem for him by naming that picture *Hope* when all he could see was hell and a quiet desperation. But then Dr. Sampson said he noticed that he had only been checking out the horizontal dimensions and relationships in that picture—how the woman was hooked up with that world on which she sat. He had failed to take into account her vertical relationships. He had looked down on the painting and had seen the war, the hunger, the distrust, and the hatred, but he had not looked above her head. He said that when he looked over her head, he saw some small notes of music moving playfully and joyfully toward heaven. And it was then that he understood why Watt had called that painting *Hope*.

See, in spite of being on a world torn by war; in spite of being on a world destroyed by hate; in spite of being on a world devastated by distrust and decimated by disease; in spite of being on a world where famine and greed were uneasy bed partners; in spite of being on a world where apartheid and apathy fed the fires of racism; in spite of being on a world where nuclear nightmare draws closer with every second; in spite of being on a ticking time bomb with her clothes in rags, her body scarred, bruised, and bleeding, and her harp all but destroyed except for that one string that was left—in spite of all these things, the woman had the audacity to hope. She had the audacity to hope and to make music and to praise God on the one string she had left.

Horizontal and Vertical Dimensions

In other words, the vertical dimension balanced out what was taking place on the horizontal dimension. That is what the audacity to hope will do. Paul said the same thing. You've got troubles? Glory in your troubles. We glory in tribulation.[4] That's the horizontal dimension. We glory in tribulation because tribulation works patience, and patience works experience, and experience works hope.[5] That's the vertical dimension. "And hope maketh not ashamed."[6]

The vertical dimension balances out what is happening on the horizontal dimension. That's the real story here in 1

Samuel:1, not the condition of Hannah's body, but the condition of Hannah's soul. On the vertical dimension she had the audacity to keep on hoping and to keep on praying when there was no visible sign on the horizontal level that what she was praying, hoping, and waiting for would ever be answered affirmatively. That which she wanted most in life had been denied to her. Yet, she kept on hoping. The gloating of Peninnah did not make her bitter; she kept on hoping when the family made its annual pilgrimage to Shiloh, the place where the ark of the covenant was kept and where the mercy seat was. There Hannah renewed her petition to God. She may have been barren in her womb, but she was fertile in her spirit. Hannah was operating in the vertical dimension. She prayed and prayed, and she prayed and kept on praying year after year after year with no answer. But she prayed on anyhow.

This particular year she prayed so fervently that Eli the priest thought she was drunk. There were no visible signs on the horizontal level to say to Hannah to keep on praying. But Paul said something about that too. Paul said to hope. The vertical dimension is what saves us, for we are saved by hope, but hope that is seen is not hope, for if we hope for that which we see not, then do we with patience wait on it.[7] That's what Isaiah meant when he said, "They who wait for the Lord shall renew their strength."[8] The vertical dimension balances out what is happening on the horizontal dimension.

There may not be any sign of a change in your individual situation, that private hell where you live that I wanted you to think about. But that's just the horizontal level. First, check out the vertical as Hannah did, and you can say with the African slaves, "Over my head, I hear music in the air. Over my head, I hear music in the air. Over my head, I hear music in the air. There must be a God somewhere."[9] Keep the vertical dimension intact, and have the audacity to hope for that child of yours. Mine came out of her experience fine; there is life after teenage parenting. Have the audacity to hope for that husband of yours, to hope for that household of yours, to hope for that homosexual of yours. Keep on praying, keep on waiting, and like my grandmama, you might be able to sing, "There's a bright side somewhere. There's a bright side somewhere. Don't you rest until you find it. There's a bright side somewhere."[10]

The Audacity to Hope

In order for a people to have taken a negative and turned it into a positive, surely somebody had to have had the audacity to hope. In order for a race held in bondage to slavery to have taken a proclamation not worth the paper it was written on and to have turned it into a proposition that produced a race full of giants, somebody had to have had the audacity to hope. Abraham Lincoln is remembered as the "Great Emancipator" of the slaves, but in reality, he did not see black Africans as equal with whites. (The issue of slavery was paramount for him because it threatened the unity of the country. The primary reason that the Civil War was fought was not to free the slaves, but to save the United States because the southern states wanted to secede and form their own nation.) But blacks had a vertical hookup with the one who made Lincoln, and because they did, with little of nothing in their hands, they kept on holding onto God's unchanging hand. They had the audacity to hope. In order for some ex-slaves to turn defeat into victory, devastation into liberation, nothing into something, no schooling into some of the finest schools in the nation, somebody had to have the audacity to hope. In order for a race despised because of its color to turn out a Martin Luther King and a Malcolm X, a Paul Giddings and a Pauli Murray, a James Baldwin and a Toni Morrison, and a preacher named Jesse, and in order to claim its lineage from a preacher named Jesus, somebody had to have the audacity to hope.

In order for Martin to hang in there when God gave him a vision of an America that one day would take its people as seriously as it had taken its politics and its military power; in order for him to hang in and keep working and keep on preaching even when all the black leaders turned against him because he had the courage to call the sin of Vietnam exactly what it was – an abomination before God – he had to have the audacity to hope.

You remember that Senator Brooke turned against Martin; Jackie Robinson turned against Martin; Carl Rowan turned against Martin; Roy Wilkins turned against Martin; the NAACP passed a resolution against Martin; the Urban League turned against Martin. It was all right for this preacher to protest against North American apartheid and segregated lunch counters, but when he dared speak the message God gave him against our racist, militaristic posture in South Vietnam and our racist involvement in South Africa, he was iced and isolated by all of the establishment blacks. And in order for him to hang in and hold on, in order for him to have the audacity to hope, he had to have a vertical hookup that assimilated Negroes had forgotten all about. It was a hookup that said "before I'd be a slave [a slave to conservative theology that enslaves and preaches love], before I'd be a slave [a slave to right-wing ignorance that wears black robes on Sunday morning and white robes on Sunday night], before I'd be a slave [a slave to white America's corporate dollars that hold and pull the purse strings of so many national black organizations], before I'd be a slave, I'd be buried in my grave, and go home to my God and be free."[11]

Martin was more than a minister and a civil rights leader. Martin was a man who integrated the buses of Montgomery and the streets of Selma, yes, but Martin also took on the unjust economic system of our country. He took on the iron-fisted military system, and he took on the unabashed racism of this country because of his vertical hookup, his audacity to hope. There were no visible signs on the horizon, yet he kept on preaching. There was nothing on the horizon to say that he should keep on hoping, but he kept on hoping anyhow; he kept the vertical dimension intact, and that is the message for us. Have the audacity to hope anyhow, no matter what you can't see. The real lesson that Hannah gives us from this chapter is how to hope when the love of God is not plainly evident.

I sat there that day listening to Frederick G. Sampson with no sign on the horizon that God was loving me or hearing my prayers. You see, it's easy for us to have hope when we can see signs and evidence all around us of how God's love is present. We can walk around singing "The Lord is blessing me right now." But when you don't know where that bright side is that my grandmama used to sing about, and you still hope, then that is the true test of a Hannah-type faith. To take that one string that you have left and have the audacity to hope, to make music and praise God on whatever it is you've got left – that's the real word from the passage and the real message from that painting that the Lord would have us hear and see.

I listen to the young people singing. They know the modern gospel numbers. They know all of Sister Winans' songs and everything that James Cleveland popularized. But they don't know some of the old songs. Until our church started singing some of those hymns on Sunday morning, they had never heard those songs. These old songs predate the *National Baptist Hymnal*; they're even too old to be in the *Gospel Pearls*. Most of you who are over thirty-five can remember "I thank you, Jesus. I thank you, Jesus. I thank you, Jesus, thank you, Lord. O, you brought me, yes, you brought me from a mighty, a mighty long way, a mighty long way."

My parents would sing that song around our house, and they would sing it at what seemed to be some of the strangest times. When the money got low and things were tight and Daddy had to take flour and add it to the beans to make them thicker, he would stir up the beans and sing "I thank you, Jesus." Or when I got in trouble and had to be punished, he'd be coming up the stairs with a razor strap in his hands singing "I thank you, Jesus."

When I go to speak at various churches, there's a nice biography on me on the back of the program and a nice blurb in the newspapers, but what these don't tell you is that at fifteen years of age I was busted for grand larceny auto theft. And the night after my father got me out of prison and took me home, I was waiting for the whipping that I knew I had coming. I heard him and my mother in their bedroom singing "I thank you, Jesus. I thank you, Jesus." Now it seemed to me that they were thanking God because we were financially in a jam; they were thanking him because we didn't have any money; they were thanking him because we didn't have enough food; or they were thanking him because I was messing up. But I was just looking at the horizontal dimension. I couldn't see the vertical hookup that my mama and my daddy had. I did not know back then that they were thanking him in advance for all that they had the audacity to hope for and for all that they believed God would answer. I did not know they were thanking him for how they hoped God would intervene and for what he would one day do for and through their son. I couldn't see that vertical dimension back then. But now, some forty years later, oh my God! I'm more crazy than they were walking around singing "I thank you, Jesus."

See, I tried living without the Lord. Fifteen wasn't the only age at which I got in trouble. When I went away to college, I thought I was grown. I didn't have to go to church anymore. I left the church. I was licensed to preach my freshman year, but my sophomore year, Chi Psi Phi. I tried living without the Lord. I was influenced by Martin King, yes, but there was this other guy named Malcolm, and I tried one brief time being a Muslim: "As salaam alaikum."[12] Anything but a Christian. I tried getting away from the Lord. But my mom and dad had the audacity to keep on praying. There was no sign on the horizon. I was acting like a complete fool. But they kept on praying, kept on hoping, kept on thanking, and right now, "Thank you, Jesus," I pastor the largest congregation in the United Church of Christ because the Lord heard their prayers!

Have the audacity to hope. Hope on anyhow. He's a good God. He touched my life and made me whole. Praise God!

Study Questions

1. Consider what it means to be on top of the world, like the woman in Watt's painting *Hope*. From your vantage point, what are the "horizontal" and "vertical" realities?

2. Should Christians ever give up hoping? What should be our response when someone is dying? Should we continue to pray for healing?

3. How can we maintain hope in the healing and loving power of God when we're faced with the realities of chronic illnesses, broken relationships, and other circumstances that God has not seen fit to change?

4. Hannah's husband, Elkanah, pleaded with her to turn from her depression, saying, "Hannah, why do you weep? And why do you not eat? And why is your heart sad? Am I not more to you than ten sons?" (1 Samuel 1:8, RSV). He seemed to think his love could substitute for her ability to be a mother, but Hannah was not looking for a substitute. Is it appropriate to seek substitutes for what we believe to be lacking in our lives? What might be the positive and negative consequences of doing so?

5. Hannah had the audacity to hope in a situation that seemed hopeless. Look at the priest's response. Because of Eli's response, what did she risk in taking her petition to God? (1 Samuel 1:12-16)

6. When we exhaust all of our human resources, and it is clear that only God can "fix" our difficult situations, what risks do we take in making our appeals to God? Because of these risks, why is it necessary that we believe that God will answer our prayers and that we trust that whatever answers we receive will be the right answers?

7. List "impossible" situations in your personal life, the life of your community, in your school, or on your job. Do you have the audacity to hope in these situations?

8. Give a testimony about something or someone that required of you the audacity to hope. What happened?

9. What is the difference between hope and false pre-

sumption? To what extent can we base our hopes on things that require the commitments and actions of other persons?

10. Think of someone who needs encouragement to have hope. Be guided by prayer in ministering to that person.

When God Is Silent

Psalm 10:1; Psalm 83:1

From the Good News translation of the Bible come two powerful lines from two different psalms, written by two different but both devastatingly honest poets. Persons who have drunk deeply from the wellsprings of life, and who know the quickening candor of the human heart at that painful and personal moment when it feels like God has abandoned us and left us all alone, feel as they do because God is silent.

The first line from the first verse of Psalm 10 (GNB) says:

Why are you so far away, O LORD?
Why do you hide yourself when we are in trouble?

Although one psalm written by David says, "In the time of trouble he shall hide me . . . ,"[1] this psalm says that when we are in trouble, God hides himself. "Why are you so far away, O LORD? Why do you hide yourself when we are in trouble?" It feels that way because God is silent.

The other line is from the first verse of Psalm 83. The *Good News Bible* reads as follows:

O God, do not keep silent;
Do not be still, do not be quiet!

When we need a word from the Lord, sometimes God is silent. When we need an answer from the throne of grace, sometimes God is silent. When we need a word of hope in a hopeless situation, sometimes God is silent. When we need a message of mercy in a messed up set of circumstances, sometimes God is silent. When we need a grace note to transpose the jangling discords and dissonance that are heard all around us, a grace note to transpose all of that into the harmonious symphony of what doth not yet appear, God is silent.

When we want God to say something – anything: yes, no, maybe so, not now, wait awhile, by-and-by – God is silent. And the psalm writer who has been there cries out, "O God, do not keep silent!"

Have you ever been there? If you haven't, just keep on living. You will get there. As much as our modern "pop" religion hates to admit it, Scripture says there are those times when God is silent. As much as this goes against the grain of our American understanding of prosperity (God giving us all of the riches we want while South Africans starve to death) and as much as it goes against our treating God as some sort of cosmic bellhop (we tell him how to hop and he just jumps there; "just ask for the gift, honey, and he gives it to you"), Scripture says there are those times when God is silent. Sometimes God is silent. God reveals himself, yes. He makes himself known to us. But God also conceals himself. Isaiah 45:15 (NRSV) says, "Truly you are a God who hides himself."

God conceals himself, and sometimes he makes himself known to us just as much, if not more, in the concealing as he does in the revealing. In fact, I am convinced that one of the things God wants us to learn from those times of silence is that God is doing some revealing of himself in the concealing of himself. He is both immanent and transcendent, both revealed and concealed. What can be learned from those times when God is silent?

In the early days of my being a full-fledged ordained pastoral minister, standing there wet behind the ears with two degrees from Howard University, and working toward a Ph.D. at the University of Chicago Divinity School, God placed in my life an old black man who became a master teacher for me. He taught me about the goodness of God,

and he taught me about the silence of God. He taught me
about those times when you feel too good, as if you are going to explode, because God is so good. And he taught me
about those times when you feel that God has left you all
alone. He was chestnut brown with dirty white hair like
snow that has been walked on. This giant of a man came
into my life like a towering pillar of strength. He had a
tongue that could be as encouraging as an angelic chorus
when it had to be or could be as discouraging as a drill ser-
geant at Parris Island in South Carolina when it had to be.
This giant was named Mr. Burns, Devereaux Burns. Mr.
Burns could speak a word and pick up your spirits whenever
he saw the need, or he could speak a word when you got too
big for your britches and cut you right back down to size.
Mr. Burns, with no degrees from Howard or the University
of Chicago, said to me one time: "Don't you let nobody turn
you around or run you away from here, Son. Don't you let
nobody tell you that you can't be black and serve and love
the Lord." He said, "Too many Negroes trying to be white as
it is; you keep on being what the Lord made you boy, and
you're gonna make it. Yes, God. You gonna make it."

Mr. Burns knew the passages from the Bible where Jesus
is described as having dark brown skin and nappy hair.[2] He
knew where the Queen of Sheba said in the Song of Solomon, "I am black and beautiful,"[3] not black *but*, but black
and beautiful. He knew the old Dr. Watts hymns from the
black church one hundred years ago, and he disrupted our
highly structured order of services anytime he felt like singing one of them. (We have an anthem and a choral response
following the invocation. Whenever the spirit moved him,
Mr. Burns would holler out, "Eyeeeeeeee love the
Lord. . . .")[4]

Mr. Burns knew the traditional gospel, from the old quar-
tets up through James Cleveland, and he loved preaching.
He was a preacher's friend. One time our youth choir was
going somewhere with me on a trip, and some of the people
who didn't like the kids' music made it clear they would not
help finance the trip. The teenagers didn't have quite
enough money, and being teenagers, they had no hope of

getting any money from any place other than their little al-
lowances. So you know what Mr. Burns did? He had himself
a quarter party in his house to raise money to send the teenagers from his church on a trip.

I have a vivid mental image of him out on his patio that
night when the party was almost over. Most of the folks had
left, and he was out there, seventy-five years old and dancing with his sixty-three-year-old wife, singing a love song to
her the whole time. And then, with tears in his eyes, he gave
me that handful of money in a big sack and said, "Tell those
children to sing till the power of the Lord comes down." He
had the wisdom and compassion to overcome the obstacles
put up by those who were acting like musical snobs.

At times like that, Mr. Burns' tongue could be like an angelic chorus, bringing from above "echoes of mercy and
whispers of love." Then, at other times, Mr. Burns could tell
you exactly what was on his mind, and he didn't care where
he was when he told you. I happened to be the recipient of
his opinion on one particular occasion. He got sick and the
doctors wanted him to have surgery, but he did not want
any surgery; he had cancer. Without the surgery, they said
he could live for about three months, maximum. With the
surgery, he could make it four or five years, maybe. It was a
difficult decision. Mr Burns said no to the surgery: "I'll go
with the max and not mess with the maybe." Then his wife
called me, and the doctors called me, and they said, "You
talk with him. He treats you like a son; he will listen to you."
So I talked to him. He listened and said yes to the surgery.
Before the operation he came home from the hospital for a
weekend to spend some time with his family and to worship
one more time with his church family.

Well, that Sunday was in the early days of my pastorate
at Trinity United Church of Christ, and the folks wanted to
be very, very sophisticated. And, as a young pastor, I was
trying to please everybody. The music committee had come
to me concerning that Sunday before Christmas and had
said they wanted a cantata rather than a sermon. So, since
this was my first year at the church, I gave in. I didn't

preach that Sunday; we had a cantata the Sunday before Christmas at the eleven o'clock service.

As folks came out of the door, smiling and shaking my hand, they said all kinds of strange things like, "You know, well, it was different [nervous chuckle], effective, moving." As I looked down that line, I saw Mr. Burns with tears in his eyes again, and I felt good. He grabbed my hand, and right there in the sanctuary, he froze that smile on my face, and he said, "Reverend, you knew I had to go up under the surgeon's knife this week. Y'all should have told me you was gonna have this mess, and I could have gone somewhere else and gotten something for my soul. Now I got to go some damn where and find me a church before I go back to the hospital. The one time I needed to hear the gospel was this Sunday." His tongue said exactly what was on his mind.

Well, my giant of a teacher did find another church to worship in that morning, and he told me about it when I went to see him before his surgery. He had his surgery, and he lived about three more years. When he got sick for that last time, he asked the doctors if he could come home to die. I went to see him a couple of times a week, and toward the end, every other day. On the Sunday before he died, I knelt by his bed and we had prayer. I called on the Lord and I asked God to have mercy.

I went back to his home on the day he was dying. When I came into his room and saw that fixed stare in his eye (I don't know if you have ever been in the face of death like that), I started praying and crying. I begged God to have mercy, and God was silent. I heard the death rattle coming from the throat of my giant. I had heard it many times during my six years in the military service: men dying and gurgling out their last few breaths; men dying who had hardly had a chance to live; men dying who had no idea why they had been fighting; men dying for a country that denied their humanity, negated their personhood, and relegated their black skins to second-class citizenship. I had heard that death rattle many times before, and when I heard it coming from the throat of that chestnut-brown man who

had been my strong tower of support in the early years of
my pastorate, I could not handle it. I cried out to God in
desperation, and God was silent.

> Why are you so far away, O LORD?
> Why do you hide yourself when we are in trouble?
> O God, do not keep silent.

And God was still silent.

I ran from Mr. Burns's room, right out of his house. I,
who could take flak; I, who could take heat; I, who could
take criticism; I, who could take smart talk, back talk, and
bad talk; I, who could take on a racist in a one-on-one, toe-to-
toe confrontation—verbal or physical (didn't matter to me);
I, who could take on one who ignorantly mishandled the
Word of God; I, who could take all that the Marine Corps
put on me, all that the Navy ran by me, and all that Aunt
Hannah's children[5] brought to me; I could not take Mr.
Burns dying and God's silence. I ran to another deacon's
home about two blocks away, and through my sobs I asked
if that deacon had ever done ministry to the dying. I explained as best I could what was happening. He went to Mr.
Burns' house, and I went out into the night alone with my
tears, alone with my fears, alone with my memories, alone
with my pain, unable to talk and with no one to talk back to
me. God was still silent.

> Why are you so far away, O LORD?
> Why do you hide yourself when we are in trouble?

My degrees from Howard and my studies at the University of Chicago did not equip me to deal with the death of
my friend and the silence of God. What was I supposed to
do, after all? I was a pastor, and this family would be looking to me to help them through what I was having trouble
getting through myself. My help (David said, "I will lift up
mine eyes unto the hills, from whence cometh my help)[6] was
not only silent but also nowhere to be found.

Job said (Job 23:3, GNB), "How I wish I knew where to

find him, and knew how to go where he is." God hides himself and is silent. Job said, "I have searched in the East, but God is not there." God hides himself and is silent. Job said, "I have not found him when I searched in the West" (23:8, GNB). God hides himself and is silent. Job said, "God has been at work in the North and the South, but still I have not seen him."[7] God hides himself and is silent.[8] Job said, ". . . The wounded and dying cry out, but God ignores their prayers." God hides himself and is silent.

Jesus said, in quoting the first verse of Psalm 22, "My God, my God, why hast thou forsaken me?" I, too, have cried desperately for help, but still it does not come. God hides himself and is silent. Psalm 22:2 (GNB) continues: "During the day I call to you, my God, but you do not answer; I call at night, but get no rest." God hides himself and is silent. My help was not only silent but also nowhere to be found.

> Why are you so far away, O LORD?
> Why do you hide yourself when we are in trouble?
> O God, do not keep silent.

And still there was no answer. Only the sad sound of my voice bouncing off the sorrow-filled night of stony silence.

When God Is Silent

What can we learn from those times when God is silent?

One of our members at Trinity was seventeen years old and had cancer—not seventy-five, not seventy-eight, but seventeen with cancer. She had had an arm amputated, and the only thing on her mind was trying to make it so she could graduate from high school before she died, while other seventeen-year-olds were running around gang-banging, not studying, and making dope. And God was silent.

Black children in South Africa can't go to school, can't find work, and have nothing to eat, while black children in Houston won't go to school, don't want to work, and expect to eat. And God is silent.

We have no money to educate our inner-city children who

happen to be black and brown, but we do have money to wage war in the Persian Gulf. We do have money to send those same black and brown children to an early and unnecessary grave, wearing the uniforms of a country that will not make funds available for making geniuses, only for making war. This country will exterminate them, but not educate them. And God is silent.

Martin gave his life for the cause of a more humane and just society and a reordering of an economic priority in a society gone insane with self-interest and sick military solutions for every problem. Twenty-two years later, none of those issues have gotten better by one iota; if anything, they have gotten worse. African Americans are still at the bottom of the economic ladder. There is a resurgence of racism. We have traded Vietnam for Grenada in the Reagan years and for Panama in the Bush years. Martin's dream has turned into a nightmare, and God is silent. What can we learn from those times when God is silent?

We Become Frustrated When God Is Silent

The first lesson I learned was the lesson of frustration. It is frustrating to want answers for life's most difficult questions, and not to have those answers forthcoming. Frustration. It is frustrating to get knocked down like Job, strung up like Jesus, picked on like Elijah, and messed over like some of you have been. It is frustrating to expect God's help and instead get only a holy hush. It is frustrating to expect solace, and instead get silence. Frustration. It is frustrating to hear no explanation and to be left alone in silence to try to figure out for ourselves what we have done to bring on that feeling of isolation.

When one of my classmates, a colleague from the University of Chicago, had cancer, I went to talk to him. Unlike Mr. Burns, this man had been sick for over twenty years, and he said, "No religious theory adequately explains why I or your friend contracted cancer. Nor do I know why I am alive and not dead like your friend." (Don has been in remission four times over the twenty years.) "That's a mystery," he said. "I have stopped seeking explanations, because we are left after all of our rational searches with an impenetrable surd. I have learned that I must believe *in spite of* rather than *because of*, if I am to believe at all."

"Christianity," this scholar said to me, "was once a doctrinal system of truths to believe and laws to obey. Fighting cancer for over twenty years has changed that," he said. "I now comprehend my faith as a faltering trust in a God I barely understand." In other words, faith is primarily relational; it is not conceptual. He concluded: "My faith now is rooted in an experience of receiving daily life as a sheer gift."

See, it is frustrating to try to piece together in your own mind what it is you're going through, to understand what it is that is happening to you, why it is you're feeling that way, while wondering all at the same time where God is, what God is doing, and why God isn't saying anything. How did God let this happen in the first place? That's too much for a human mind to try to comprehend. The mind is put on a mode that I call "overload." Like a computer, the mind in this mode will not compute. And it leads to frustration. Look at Job out on his ash heap, asking questions and getting no answers because God was silent. "Oh, that I knew where I might find him!"[9] Frustration.

Look at Elijah underneath his juniper tree, wishing that he could die, and God was silent. "It's too much, LORD . . . Take away my life; I might as well be dead!"[10]

Look at Jesus out on Calvary, with undeserved punishment, unrelenting pain, and God was silent. "My God, my God, why hast thou forsaken me?"[11] That's frustrating.

Look at Martin in his kitchen, late in the midnight hour, trying to hear from heaven, trying to get some answers, some response, with his family under the threat of death and the whole movement seemingly unraveling at the seams, and God is silent. That's frustrating — frustrating to hear no response and to be left alone in silence to try to figure out for ourselves what we have done to bring on that feeling of isolation. That's frustrating.

Why are you so far away, O LORD?
Why do you hide yourself when we are in trouble?

Then, sometimes the situation of silence is compounded by what I like to call the "Mothers from Missouri." Do you know who they are? They're the "show me" folks: "I've got to see something before I believe it." Job had them — Mothers from Missouri. He had friends who wanted to see rationally what the problem was. "Show me. You know you've done something, Job. I know that's right!"[12] And God was silent. That's frustrating.

Elijah had those Mothers from Missouri. Jezebel said, "Well your God is so tough, huh? You've got to show me, 'cause I am going to do to you what they're telling me you did to my prophets. Now show me your God can stop me."[13] And God was silent. That's frustrating. Martin had them too. They tracked him in and out of the movement. That's frustrating. Jesus had them. The crowd passing by the cross and one of the thieves hanging beside him on a cross also said, "You're bad. Show me. Save yourself and us, too. Come on down off the cross. You saved others. What's the problem, now? You trust in God; let's see what God's going to do for you now."[14] And God was silent. That's frustrating.

The same Psalm 22 that Jesus quoted as he hung on the cross, says in verses 7 and 8 (GNB):

All who see me make fun of me;
  They stick out their tongues and shake their heads.
"You relied on the LORD," they say.
  "Why doesn't he save you?
If the LORD likes you,
  why doesn't he help you?"

The Mothers from Missouri say, "I want to see something. Show me." And God is silent. That's frustrating. Then there's the ultimate frustration that even if God were to break God's silence, we wouldn't be able to understand anyhow.

My thoughts are not your thoughts,
  neither are your ways my ways, says the LORD.
For as the heavens are higher than the earth,

so are my ways higher than your ways
and my thoughts than your thoughts."¹⁵

The first lesson I learned when God was silent was the lesson of frustration.

In the Silence, God Communicates with Us

We are a noise-oriented culture. We get up in the morning to clock radios; we turn on the television for "Good Morning America," the morning news, the weather report, and traffic reports. We ride to work listening to the radio. Some of us like that elevator music; the saints listen to the gospel station; other folks like that boom shaka laka laka as they ride to work. And do you realize that what we call "soft" music in our noise-oriented culture has become known as elevator music because we don't want to be in the elevator alone, in silence. We even have background music in department stores to help us shop until we drop.

We have music in the movies to let us know what's going on (chase music, love scene music, fight music). When I was growing up, everybody in the movie theater knew when the Lone Ranger was coming. We are such a noise-oriented culture that children, teenagers, young adults, and adults walk around with something called a "Walkman" to keep away the deadening threat of silence. And in case those of you who are parents or grandparents of teenagers haven't noticed recently, our culture has fallen in love with something else. It's not called music anymore; it's called "rap."

We are a noise-oriented culture. We come home in the evening and turn on the television just for the background noise. We even have a timer on the TV to turn itself off after it has put us to sleep. We are such a noise-oriented culture that sometimes God has to use silence to communicate with us to get our attention. Sometimes God wants us to shut up so we can hear, and God will keep silent to get us to listen more attentively.

Listen to our prayers and hear just how foolish and selfish some of them are. Listen carefully to hear what it is God

has already said but that we in our haste might have
missed. Listen to remember that sometimes God does not
speak in the thunder; sometimes God does not speak in the
earthquake; sometimes God does not speak in the storm,
but out of the whirlwind in a still small voice that you can't
hear when there is a lot of noise around you.[16] God will use
silence to communicate with us.

The second lesson I learned was the lesson of communication. And, oddly enough, in pastoral counseling one of the
things they teach us, and that we teach others about com-
municating, is the difficult art of listening—shutting up
and being silent and listening—not just being quiet while
the other person is talking and waiting for him or her to
take a breath so that you can jump in to tear up what he or
she is saying, but actually being silent and listening to what
the other person is saying. From my own prayer life over the
past twenty years in the ordained ministry, I am convinced
that God will use silence to listen to us and to engage us in
the high and holy art of communication.

God will use silence to communicate with us. Psalm 22:2
(GNB) says: "I call at night but get no rest. You may remember the song from the church tradition: "In the stillness
of the midnight, sacred secrets he'll unfold." God will use silence to communicate with us. What did the prophet say?
"The LORD is in his holy temple; let all the earth keep silence
before him."[17]

Let God's Silence Signal Your Anticipation

The first lesson I learned was the lesson of frustration;
the second lesson I learned was the lesson of communication, but the ultimate lesson I learned was the lesson of anticipation: learning how to wait with expectancy although
you can neither hear from heaven at that moment nor see
what God is doing at that moment. Number one: God is still
on the throne. Number two: God is doing something about
it in his own way and in his own time. (God works on his
timetable, not ours.) And, number three: We will understand it better by and by.

Anticipation. God is fixing it right now, even though I

can't see how. Anticipation. While I am trying to figure it out, God has already worked it out. Anticipation. Job was out on his heap of degradation. God already had a plan of restoration. Learn how to wait with the expectancy that God is doing something about it. When those Mothers from Missouri come by telling you to show them something, you tell them, "We walk by faith, not by sight."[18]

I believe in the sun, even when it is not shining, and I believe in God, even when God is silent. Anticipation. Faith is relational, not conceptual: "It doth not yet appear what we shall be. . . ."[19] We believe *in spite of*, not *because of*. While Elijah was out under his juniper tree wondering how, God already had seven thousand more who would not bow.[20] "Faith is the assurance of things hoped for, the conviction of things not seen."[21] Learn how to wait with the expectancy that God is doing something about it right now.

While I was out in the night sobbing about my friend Mr. Burns, being in pain that I could not help, God had already taken my friend to a place where there is no more pain, there is no more sorrow, there are no more tears, no more crying, and no more dying. Anticipation: learning how to wait with the expectancy that God is still on the throne. While Martin was being gunned down, God was already waiting in the wings getting ready to do some lifting up. God has lifted up all kinds of leaders since Martin was here. And sometimes we're so fixated on what Martin did that we can't see what God is doing.

I was in Cuba, where I've gone three times with the Black Theology Project for the Martin Luther King Annual Theological Seminar. A lot of us from North America don't know that there are Christians in Cuba. They not only have Christians, but for the last twenty-one years, they have had an annual theological seminar on the life, work, and ministry of Martin Luther King. When they opened the Martin Luther King, Jr., Center they honored me by asking me to deliver the message. Well, I'd preached in Cuba before, and in Nicaragua and Honduras. When you preach in a foreign country, you say two or three sentences and then let the translator repeat them for the people. You say a little bit more; the

translator says a little bit more. In Cuba it was very inter-
esting because the translators were all from the Marxist
persuasion, and some of them were members of the Communist party. A lot of the language about the church and faith
in God and the Bible was alien to them.

The translator assigned to us was a little girl younger
than my daughter. She had never been on the inside of a
church up to that week when we arrived in Cuba, so she
needed the same thing the seminar required—that we mail
our papers so they could be translated ahead of time and so
that difficult terms could be figured out. She said, "I need a
copy of your message so I can translate it and have all the
words correct." I said, "I can't give it to you until God gives
it to me." She said, "But, sir, your service is Sunday, and it's
Friday." I said, "I know, and when I get it, I will give it to
you." I added, "I don't want you to get confused, because
sometimes there are some things too hot for paper, and
you're going to be looking around trying to figure out where
I am in that manuscript, and I'm not going to be on that
manuscript. But I'm not going to say anything unusual or
too hard. I know your language."

But she said, "You don't understand. I don't know the
church." So we talked. We talked about the Lord Jesus
Christ. She had never heard about the Lord Jesus Christ as
a personal savior. She had heard about the atrocities of the
Catholic church and had seen how the church had oppressed
the poor in her country. But she had never heard of A.M.E.
or A.M. E. Zion[22] or National Baptists, unincorporated or
incorporated. She didn't know any of that. She had never
been in the church. I kept asking her about her own faith,
and she kept talking about Marx and Lenin. I asked her
about Jesus Christ, who is the King of kings, and she just
never knew what I was talking about. She just could not
understand what I was saying. We also talked about the different artists of Europe and the different periods in art that
she had learned about in school and that I had studied as
well in humanities courses.

Well, I did give her the manuscript that Sunday afternoon, and she had about four hours to look at it. When I
stood up to preach, I just had a feeling in terms of anticipa-

tion that God was going to do something in that sermon and something in that message for that church. I didn't know what it was; I just expected God to act. I started preaching, and she translated; and I preached, and she translated. Well, sure enough, we got down to the end of the message, and the Lord gave me something that wasn't on the paper. I started talking about a picture that my translator had seen. It's a picture of Mephistopheles and Dr. Faust. It's called *Checkmate*. You may have seen it. It depicts the devil Mephistopheles sitting on one side of the chessboard and Faust sitting on the other side. All of the pieces are gone except the king and the queen and one little rook for Faust. The devil's got him cornered, and he has a smirk on his face to symbolize what had happened when Faust sold his soul to the devil.[23] There are no more moves, and Faust is in serious trouble. Mephistopheles is just waiting for him and saying "checkmate."

That painting hangs in the gallery in London. About ten years ago, a tour group going through the gallery was looking at the picture, and the tour guide was telling the group how much the picture cost, who painted it, what the different textures were, how long it took to paint it, and so forth, and then they moved on. But nobody noticed that when the group moved on, one person stayed right there in front of that painting and kept staring and pacing back and forth. I said that and my translator translated it. And the man in the museum was looking at the painting, and he kept looking at the painting. She translated that. As he paced back and forth, the group moved away and was two corridors away when all of a sudden, coming through those marble halls they heard this man hollering at the top of his lungs, "It's a lie! It's a lie! The king has another move." And she translated that. Nobody knew that the man in the museum was the international chess champion from Russia. As a master, he could see what the ordinary chess player could not see: there was another move for the king. And the same thing is true when it comes to the King of kings. The King always has another move.

On April 4, 1968, didn't it look like the game was all over? But it was a lie. The King had another move. On Friday afternoon they put him in the ground, but it was a lie. The King had another move.

While I was preaching and as she was translating, I noticed that the group from North America, including Dexter Wise and Wyatt Tee Walker,[24] had stopped looking at me. They were watching her and waving handkerchiefs and saying, "Go ahead, baby. Go ahead, baby." And I'm the one preaching the sermon. When I looked over at her, I realized (because I had studied Spanish for six years) that she wasn't translating one word I was saying. She had accepted the Lord Jesus Christ and was over there praising him.

"¡Gracias, Dios! ¡Gracias, Dios! El rey tiene siempre otra movida!" The king always has another move! Always anticipate that God will make a move that we cannot see or understand. Come unto Jesus while you have time.

Study Questions

1. As a man lay dying at a hospice, the clinical social worker was overheard to say that death was harder for Christians because they believe God will save them from their illnesses. In fact, several of his brothers in Christ claimed his healing and refused to believe that he would die. When God is silent, as he was in this case, is the Christian who knows the Word of God more advantaged or disadvantaged than the Christian who doesn't or the non-Christian?

2. How can Romans 8:28 apply to the frustration that we experience when God is silent?

3. Many Christians pray regularly for the end of the scourge of illicit drugs in our nation. Does it seem that this prayer is falling upon deaf ears? Do you think that 2 Chronicles 7:14 explains why this prayer hasn't been affirmatively answered? Why? Why not?

4. Apply question 3 to other needs, such as cures for can-

cer, diabetes, and AIDS; the end of the senseless violence in our streets; and the provision of affordable health insurance for all citizens.

5. Look at questions 3 and 4. Feel free to add other concerns. Form discussion groups to address the frustrations that these issues cause in the family, the community, and the nation. Address this question: Is God really silent, or are we being too noisy to hear or too disobedient to do what God is instructing us to do?" Are there other reasons why these prayers seemingly go unanswered?

6. What would be some of the spiritual benefits to us of lessening the noise in our lives? What are some practical ways to establish quiet times?

7. This sermon tells about a time of spiritually motivated anticipation as Dr. Wright was about to preach in Cuba. Have you ever had a similar feeling that something from God was about to take place? Share this experience with others.

8. Consider two poignant stories in this sermon: one about an old man who is dying and the other about a young woman who finds new life in Jesus Christ. The first story illustrates the frustration caused by God's silence. The second story illustrates the concept of anticipation. Did one of these stories grip you more than the other? If so, which one, and why?

9. Look at the texts for this sermon, as well as Psalm 22 and the documented passages from the Book of Job. Using these Scriptures, and others of your own choosing, write a short essay entitled "The Biblical Witness to the Silence of God."

10. A Negro Spiritual asks, "Tell me how did you feel when you come out the wilderness, leaning on the Lord?" How did you feel when God's silence was broken and God blessed you and/or revealed something to you?

Faith in a Foreign Land

Daniel 6:1-10

I want you to consider a familiar passage of Scripture as found in the *Good News Bible* (Today's English Version).

> By the rivers of Babylon we sat down;
>   there we wept when we remembered Zion.
> On the willows near by
>   we hung up our harps.
>   ...
> Those who captured us told us to sing;
>   They told us to entertain them:
>   "Sing us a song about Zion."
> How can we sing a song to the LORD
>   in a foreign land?"[1]

Come back with me in time, way back to a faraway place, and stand for a moment shoulder-to-shoulder with another people in another place, another time, and another predicament; a people in a predicament of pain nothing like yours, nothing like anything you've experienced or could even imagine. Just quietly stand and feel. Don't say a word; just let their lives speak to your life, their spirits to your spirit. Not even a whisper, for they will fall strangely silent if they detect a stranger in their midst. Just stand where they stand for a moment and listen.

These are an African people, who for the most part are shepherds. They're a relatively peaceful people. They love music. Music permeates the fabric of their lives. They sing

when a new life is conceived; they sing when a new baby is
born; they sing while they work; they sing as they play.
They do hand jive and hambone.[2] They are famous for their
rhyming and their rapping, and you ought to see and hear
their little girls jump Double-Dutch.[3] Such rhythms and
made-up rhyming you've never heard.

They sing at weddings; they sing at funerals; some of
them sing out their sermons; some of them sing out their
prayers. They love music. Music permeates the fabric of
their lives. They go into church saying, "Make a joyful noise
unto the LORD all ye lands. Serve the LORD with gladness.
Come before his presence with singing" (Psalm 100:1-2,
KJV).

And drums? You ain't heard no drums until you hear this
people on the drums. They have drums for church, drums
for play; they have talking drums, male and female drums,
and some drums you can hear in the summertime when the
weather is warm, sort of beating the beat that makes even
the deadbeats want to start moving. Music permeates every
fabric of their lives.

And dance? You ain't seen no dancing. They just make
up dancing on the spur of the moment, unchoreographed,
unrehearsed. Music is like the air that surrounds every living thing for them. They are engulfed by music from the cra-
dle to the grave. They make up impromptu songs to
celebrate everything and anything – from a victory in battle, to a religious processional, to lovemaking between a
man and a woman. These people love music and they love
life. They love the deep things of life and the simple things
of life, the things that give life meaning and the things that
make life beautiful.

These are a profound people, a proud people, and a praying people. It was these people who built the pyramids,
which our western minds, for all of their sophistication, still
cannot figure out. It was these people who created the first
cultures and developed the first civilizations on earth. It
was these people, black of skin and wooly of hair, who gave
to the world Pythagorean mathematics,[4] and the cosmology
of Thales of Miletus.[5] It was these people, with their music
and their rhythms who gave the world Epicurean material-

ism,[6] Platonic idealism,[7] Judaism, Christianity, and Islam. These are a profound people, a proud people, and a praying people.

A People in Exile

But something has happened to these proud people. Stand here and listen. Let's see if we can learn what happened that makes them seem so different. Over here they're singing, and from the song they're singing, it sounds like they're in exile – snatched away from the homes they built, the places where they lived, and the sites that they loved; in exile – pulled away from their places of worship, where they met God and mysteriously felt God's awesome presence; in exile – taken away from the villages and towns where they grew up, fell in love, got married, settled down, started families, and began building on their dreams.

No longer are they in charge of their own lives; no longer are they in control of their daily activities; no longer are they able to sleep as husbands and wives, parents and children. And in some places no longer are they even considered to be human beings. Now they're looked upon as things, pieces of property, as "its," but never as "thous." They're toys to be played with, but never equals to be talked to; they're pieces to lie with, but never persons to be reckoned with or reconciled to; they're monkeys (if you listened to one racist guest who appeared on the "Oprah Winfrey Show"); they're nobodies, nothings, less than fully human, three-fifths of a person. In exile they are made fun of and mated like cattle. The song they sing sounds like a song sung from the bowels of exile. Listen to it:

Sometimes I feel like a motherless child, a long way from home.

In exile! Listen!

By the rivers of Babylon we sat down;
    there we wept when we remembered Zion.
On the willows near by
    we hung up our harps.

Those who loved music refused to sing in exile.

Those who captured us told us to sing;
   They told us to entertain them.
   "Sing us a song about Zion."

In exile this pained people, 'buked and scorned, cried out,

How can we sing a song to the LORD
   in a foreign land?

What has happened to this proud people is that they are
in exile, and sometimes it's hard to make merry when you
are being messed over and messed on. Wait a minute. Move
away from the singing for just a moment and stand over
here where the griot, the storyteller, is holding forth, weav-
ing together a message with meaning, simultaneously giving us narration and interpretation. Listen to see if we can
learn what happens to a people who are forced to live in a
foreign land.

Stripped of Their Names

The griot is talking about his ancestors, a man named
Daniel and some friends of his who lived in exile. Early on in
this tale (1:7), the griot tells us about one of the first things
that happens to a people in exile. The chief official gave
them new names: Belteshazzar, Shadrach, Meshach, and
Abednego. The empire of today—those with brutal force,
naked power, superior military might and, from time to
time, those with somebody who is not wrapped too tight in
the executive office; those who are drunk with power and
mad with megalomania; the commander-in-chief of the im-
perial forces, the empire, strips the exiles of their names.

Daniel, Hananiah, Mishael, and Azariah, all of whom
were from the tribe of Judah, were given new names by the
empire. Daniel was given the name Belteshazzar. Hananiah
was given the name Shadrach. Mishael was given the name
Meshach, and Azariah was given the name Abednego. Centuries after the Bible story, people from the continent of Af-

rica—places that today are the countries of Senegal, Guinea-Bissau, Gambia, Sierra Leone, Liberia, Cote D'Ivoire, Ghana, Togo, Benin, Nigeria, Cameroon, Equatorial Guinea, Gabon, Congo, Zaire, and Angola, were given new names by the empire: Negro, Negrito, Moreno, Prieta, Negress, Nigra, Nigger, Colored, Black, Coons, Sambo, Jungle Bunny, Boy, Girl, Uncle and Mammy. The empire stripped the exiles of their names and imposed its own names upon them so that five or six generations later the original names were lost to memory except for the griot's, and the only names the exiles refer to are the names given by the empire.

When you take away a person's name, you take away his or her history. My name has a history to it; I did not choose it. It was selected for me by my ancestors, parents, and grandparents long before I was conscious of their decision and what went into that decision. My name has a history. I have a grandson. My son-in-law and my daughter selected my grandson's name long before that moment when we stood in that birthing room together and I got the shock of my life. In that birthing room the nurse said to my son-in-law, "Have you picked out a name for your son?" And he turned around, grinned at me, and said, "His name is Jeremiah." My grandson's name has a history. Your name has a history, like John's name, Jesus' name, Samuel's name, and Daniel's name. They all have a history. They mean something. Daniel's name means "God is my judge." Samuel's name means "ask of God" or "name of God." John means "Yahweh has been gracious," and if you don't believe he has been gracious, ask Zechariah and Elizabeth.[8]

Hananiah also means "God has been gracious." Azariah means "Yahweh has helped." Mishael means "Who is like God?"[9] and Jesus means "Yahweh is salvation." Names have a meaning; names have a history. Wrapped up in a person's name is who he is, what family she came from, and how God has blessed that particular family by his grace in a particular manner.

No African would just willy-nilly change his or her name because each name has a history to it. The Africans in North American chattel slavery sang "I told Jesus it would

be all right if he changed my name," but they didn't change
their names, because wrapped up in their names was their
history. They sang "written down my name"; they sang
"Hush, somebody's calling my name"; they sang "I've got a
new name over in Glory, and it's mine, all mine." But no African ever willingly changed his or her own name, because
that would be like telling their mamas, their daddies, and
their ancestors to go to hell, and that's most uncharacteris-
tic of Africans.

Stripped of Their History

The North American slave owners, those "Babylonians,"
prototypes of the empire and the imperialistic mind-set that
disregards anything everybody else has ever done, did away
with the natives' names in an attempt to take away their history. As Chancellor Williams of Howard University puts it
in his question posed from a Sumer legend: "What became
of the black people of Sumer?" the traveler asked the old
man (for ancient records show that the people of Sumer were
black). "What happened to them? Ah," the old man sighed,
"They lost their history, so they died." As Dr. Ofori Atta
Thomas of the Interdenominational Theological Center
puts it, "They forgot their story." They lost their history, so
they died. Our children don't know our story. Any people
who lose their story are a dead people. And the established
authority, the empire, knows that, so it makes every deliberate attempt to take away the exiles' history. The empire tells
them that they have no history prior to the Babylonians in-
troducing them to civilization; the empire tells them outright lies and blatant distortions so that they will disown
any linkage that they once had with Africa, and they become more Babylonian than the Babylonians.

If you downgrade where the exiles' came from and what
they were once called, the grandchildren and great-grand-
children don't want to have anything to do with their history, and they embrace the culture of the "Babylonians."
They walk around with Babylonian hairstyles, Babylonian
clothes styles, Babylonian lifestyles, Babylonian ghetto

blasters to their ears, and Babylonian cocaine monkeys on
their backs. Yo, ya know what I'm sayin'? We can out-
Babylonian the Babylonians. In a foreign land, there is a deliberate attempt to take away the exiles' history and replace
it with Babylonian history.

The Babylonians told the exiles such things as "In 592
Nebuchadnezzar sailed the ocean blue. (Ask the average African American child when Africans came to this country,
and you get a blank stare. Ask them when Columbus discovered America. "Fourteen ninety-two." Columbus didn't
discover America; he got lost in the Virgin Islands looking
for India. The Indians discovered him.) Or the Babylonians
told the exiles things such as: "In 586 when your ancestors
were carried away into slavery, that was the best thing that
ever happened to them, because through the goodness of
the prejudiced Babylonian God, they were exposed to culture, literature, philosophy and fine arts, serious music and
classical music." In a foreign land there is a deliberate attempt to take away an exile's history.

At our church during our seminarians' training, we
looked at the tape that Dr. John Kinney, of Virginia Union
University School of Theology, did at the Hampton Ministers' Conference. He was telling us that that's how oppressors deal with marginalized people. The oppressors
subsume them under a larger history, so that they can make
the oppressed believe that they have never done anything.
It's how some white folks trivialize black folks; they tell
them that nothing they've done is important.

First they took their names so that they could take away
their history – who they were and where they came from and
how they got here. Listen to the griot as he tells Daniel's
story. First (1:7), he tells how the empire took their names;
then (1:4, 17) he tells us that Ashpenaz was to teach them to
read and write in the Babylonian language. Verse 17 says
God gave the four young men knowledge and skill in literature and philosophy. The empire stripped the exiles of their
heritage. They were methodically taught how to read and
write in the Babylonian language. Anyone who studies a
foreign language knows that one of the first things you have

to learn if you are going to learn the language fluently is
how to think in that language. While you are learning to
think in somebody else's language, your heritage is slowly
taken away. For three years, 365 days a year, Daniel, Hananiah, Mishael, and Azariah were schooled and skilled in the
knowledge of Babylonian literature and philosophy.

The African exiles who came to North America also were
expected to learn the culture of their empire – their "Babylon." African Americans educated in this country have forgotten what their African forebears had created – the oral
traditions and the written traditions. In fact, the "Babylonian" curriculum doesn't even include any African authors.
There are just a token few "Afro-Babylonian" hybrids accepted into the canons. These exiles became schooled in
Babylonian literature, from *Beowulf* to Virginia Wolfe, and
their heritage was wickedly wiped away from the tissues of
their memory banks. They became skilled in Babylonian
philosophy from Descartes to Meister Eckhart, from Immanuel Kant to Jean Paul Sartre, from existentialism to nihilism, from the dialectical materialism of Karl Marx to the
wissenschaftlichkeit of Martin Heidegger.[10] They became
skilled in Babylonian philosophy, and their heritage was de-
monically destroyed in the devious process.

Children of these African exiles are drilled in old Babylonian literature, middle Babylonian literature, Chaucerian
Babylonian literature, Elizabethan Babylonian literature,
Shakespearean Babylonian literature, seventeenth-century
metaphysical Babylonian literature, eighteenth-century
classical Babylonian literature, the nineteenth-century romantic Babylonian writers, and they do not know a thing
about one of their writers, because after all, their writers
never wrote what could be called serious or classical literature. Their heritage has been taken away from them.

From the African heritage, there are countless powerful
writers. One of them, Gabriel Setiloane, who taught at the
University of Capetown, is a pastor and a poet. You probably can't even go to some of our black colleges and universities to take a course where you can learn about Setiloane, a
South African black man. I recommend one poem called "I
Am an African."

This meditation is written in the characteristic style of 'African Praise Songs' (Lithoko) which the Southern African recites before a Chief on important occasions. Sometimes a man will sing praises of himself also, telling of some strong personal experience, such as a battle, in former days, while today it might be about working in the mines or a long sojourn in a strange land. —G.S.

They call me African;
African indeed am I;
Rugged son of the soil of Africa,
Black as my father, and his before him;
As my mother and sisters and brothers, living and gone from this
    world.

They ask me what I believe . . . my faith.
Some even think I have none
But live like the beasts of the field . . . . .

'What of God, the Creator
Revealed to mankind through the Jews of old,
The YAHWEH: I AM
Who has been and ever shall be?
Do you acknowledge him?'

My fathers and theirs, many generations before,
Knew him.
They bowed the knee to him
By many names they knew him,
And yet 'tis he *the One and only God* —
They called him:
UVELINGQAKI: The First One
                Who came ere ever anything appeared;
UNKULUNKULU: The BIG BIG ONE,
                So big indeed that no space could ever
                    contain him;
MODIMO: Because his abode is far up in the sky.

They also knew him as MODIRI:
        For he has made all;
and LESA: The spirit without which the breath of man cannot
    be.

But, my fathers, from the mouths of their fathers, say
That this God of old shone
With a brightness so bright
It blinded them . . . Therefore . . .
He hid himself, UVELINGQAKI,
That none should reach his presence . . .
Lest they die, (for pity flowed in his heart).
Only the fathers who are dead come into his presence,
Little gods bearing up the prayers and supplications
Of their children to the Great Great God . . .*

That is one of the writings from the African heritage not included in almost any of the "Babylonian" curriculum — the curriculum that is accepted by the "establishment," the white educational system. In a foreign land there is the deliberate and devious attempt to take away the exile's heritage and replace it with a fabricated "Babylonian" heritage that distorts truths and tells outright lies. It is done so methodically and so thoroughly that after several generations you have African exiles paying homage to Hippocrates as the father of medicine, when clearly the African Imhotep discovered and practiced medicine centuries before Hippocrates was born. You have African exiles who know nothing at all about the Africans who were performing cataract surgery a thousand years before the birth of Hippocrates.[11] You will have African exiles who think that unless the Babylonians said it, it ain't true; unless Babylonians wrote it, it ain't right; unless the Babylonians made it, it ain't gonna work.

They Couldn't Take Away Their Faith

In a foreign land an identity crisis is created in a deliberate attempt to first take away the exiles' history and then to completely destroy the exiles' heritage. But as the griot continues to talk about what happens to folk in a foreign land, those forced to live there in exile, there is something else

* "I AM AN AFRICAN" first appeared in FRONTIER MAGAZINE of the Church in Society (London), No. 3, October 1969.

that he says about Daniel that causes his listeners to stir just a little bit. It seems as though the Babylonians went too far when they tried the ultimate thing that Babylonians try, and that is to take away an exile's religion. It seems as though they overstepped their bounds and did not understand how faith in a foreign land has a tenacity that defies description.

Let's let the griot tell his story. The griot says that Nebuchadnezzar's son, Belshazzar, had a banquet.[12] At his banquet he brought out sacred objects, which had been stolen from the temple in Jerusalem, and defiled them by pouring wine in those dedicated and consecrated bowls and cups. In the midst of his party a human hand from out of nowhere appeared and started writing on the wall. It wrote *"mene, mene, tekel,"* and *"parsin"* (Daniel 5:25, RSV). And nobody could translate those words except Daniel, who interpreted it like this: *"mene,* God has numbered the days of your kingdom and brought it to an end; *tekel,* you have been weighed in the balances and found wanting; *peres* (singular of parsin), your kingdom is divided and given to the Medes and Persians" (5:26-28, RSV). That's what Daniel said, and that same night (it's something how the Lord works) Belshazzar, who desecrated those things taken from the temple, was killed; and Darius the Mede seized the royal power (as Daniel had said).

When Darius took office, he divided his empire into 120 provinces, and he put a governor in charge of each province. Over the governors he put three supervisors: Daniel and two others. And the supervisors only had one job: looking out after the king's interests. Daniel, like Joseph, rose from a position of nothing to a position of prominence in a foreign land, only Daniel did better. Daniel showed very quickly that exile or no exile, minority or culturally deprived, or any other label they wanted to pin on him, he could do better than all of the other supervisors and governors put together.

Daniel was sort of like a Doug Williams in a Super Bowl or a Martin King in the ministry or a Toni Morrison in the field of literature or a Ron McNair in the space program. He

was like a Thurgood Marshall on the Supreme Court or a
Michael Jordan or a Magic Johnson on the basketball court.
He was like a Luther Vandross or a Stevie Wonder in the
field of music or a Bo Jackson on the baseball and football
fields. He was like a Jackie Joyner-Kersee on a track, or a
Melanie Lawson on a news assignment in Panama.[13]

He was like a Carl Lewis or an Edwin Moses in a foot race
or like a Jesse Louis Jackson in a presidential race. Daniel
could do better than all of them put together. And because
he was so outstanding, the king considered putting him in
charge of the whole empire (6:3), and that's when the "stuff"
started. Those who are inferior can't stand those who are superior, especially when those who are superior are of a despised race, a race that everybody has been taught does not
have the mental equipment to be superior. They tried their
best to find something wrong with what Daniel was doing,
but they couldn't, because he was honest and he was reli-
able.

So they said to one another, "We're not going to be able to
pin anything on him unless it's in connection with this religion of his." You see, they had taken away his history and
his name and had called him Belteshazzar. They had taken
away his heritage and taught him Babylonian literature,
language and philosophy. But when they tried the ultimate
take-away — when they tried to take away his religion — they
did what all oppressors do: they tried to take away his hope.
But Daniel had the audacity to hope. When they tried to
take away his hope, they found out that their trying was in
vain.

First, they made up a lie and told the king, "Everybody,
Your Honor, Your Majesty, all of us [that's a lie; they were
including Daniel] including Daniel have come to this agreement. . . ." Then they told the king what their agreement
was: "You ought to sign this order which says that nobody
can ask anything of any man or any god for thirty days, and
if they do, they'll be put in a pit." Then they got the king to
sign the order and went to spy on Daniel to see what he was
going to do. They knew that his religion was a way of life for
him. They knew that he prayed to the God of his foreparents

three times a day. They knew that come hell or high water, problems or protocol, this man of faith was a praying man, and he was going upstairs to his prayer room to throw open his windows toward Jerusalem and call upon the name of the Lord. They knew that morning, noon, and night – every day that the good Lord sent – this brother, whom they couldn't stand, was going to be down on his knees saying, "Thank you for another day. Thank you for another night's sleep. Thank you for being my God in a foreign land, just like you are my God in my homeland." They knew that decree or no decree, royal order or no royal order, this man who believed in the power of prayer, this man whose hope was in the Holy One of Israel, would be in that window, hollering, "Father, I stretch my hands to thee. No other help I know."

So they ran as soon as the order was signed to see what God's servant would do. But, verse 10 says they could not take away his hope. When Daniel learned that the order had been signed, he went home and there, just as he had always done, Daniel knelt down at that open window and prayed. You don't pray based upon what a king says; you pray based upon your relationship with the King of kings. Whenever you feel like calling on him, you call on him; you pray. Not when the "empire" says pray. You pray every time you feel the spirit moving in your heart.

When Daniel knelt down and prayed to God, maybe he called him Yahweh; maybe he called him Joshua, "Yahweh is salvation"; maybe he called him Miqveh,[14] "the one hope, upon whom Israel is waiting"; maybe he called him Uvelingqaki, "the first one who came e'er anything appeared. Maybe he called him Unkulunkulu,[15] "so high you can't get over him, so low, you can't get under him, so wide you can't get around him"; maybe he called him Modimo, whose abode "is far up in the sky." Maybe he called him Modiri,[16] "for he has made all." Maybe he called him Lesa, the *ruah*, the *pneuma*,[17] the breath of God without which we could not live. Maybe he called him the God of Abraham and Sarah. Maybe he called him Mary's Baby or Gehazi's Judge.[18] Maybe he called him what my grandparents used to call him: Rock in a weary land, Shelter in the time of storm.

Maybe he called him Joshua's Battleaxe,[19] Jeremiah's Fire,[20] or Ezekiel's Wheel.[21] But whatever he called him, the message was the same to that listening community, and that message still is, "Hold onto your faith, even in a foreign land. Hold onto the hope that is within you, the hope that maketh not ashamed. Hold onto God's unchanging hand, no matter how hard the circumstances are around you or how they may change." Say like Daniel, and like the African said in slavery, "Yes, there is trouble all over this world, but I ain't gonna lay my 'ligion down."

Folks may mess with your history and make it hard for you to uncover it. They may mess with your heritage and cause you to forever see yourself through the tainted lenses of somebody else, but don't let go of your hope. Hold on to the faith that your mama had; hold on to the faith that your daddy had. Your faith will give you transporting power. It will carry you through dark days and lonely nights. It will give you transcending power by which you will rise above the muck and mire all around you. It will give you transforming power that will change not only you, but those around you, too. Hold on to your faith, even in a foreign land.

Don't let go of the hope that sustains you, no matter how dark the night, no matter how steep the mountain, no matter how deep the valley. Don't let go of the hope that Dr. Watts calls our hope for years to come.[22] No matter how difficult the circumstances, no matter how vicious the enemy, don't let go of your hope. Get up in the morning saying, "My hope is built on nothing less than Jesus' blood and righteousness." Go to bed at night saying, "I dare not trust the sweetest frame, but wholly lean on Jesus' name." Don't let go of your hope, no matter how high up you go on the "Babylonian" ladder.

You see, some of us have been taught this thing all wrong by some "Babylonians." They taught a lot of us that the higher up you go, the more soft and sophisticated you are supposed to become. We get one or two degrees from the "Babylonian" educational system, and we get "right cultured" and "right quiet." We're too sophisticated to say,

"Thank you, Jesus." We're too assimilated to wave our hands. We're too acculturated to praise God anyhow. I know what I'm talking about because I have been there.

But Daniel, who had gone all the way up the ladder as high as he could, threw open his windows and hollered out as loudly as he could. You see, the higher up you go, the louder you're supposed to holler. Don't get too proud to praise the Lord. Hold on to your faith. You can become a dean or a president, head or CEO of a corporation, but don't let go of a balm in Gilead.

There was a time when I didn't understand this. My mama used to be an embarrassment to me. My mama finished college at an earlier age than Martin Luther King finished. She had a master's degree at eighteen and a second master's at twenty-one. She earned a Ph.D. from the University of Pennsylvania, and my mama, with all of that education, would say every time somebody preached or prayed, "Well! Well! Well!" See the "Babylonians" taught me you were supposed to be laid back and cool; you don't make comments when someone's preaching. That's how I used to be. Oh, but when God touched my life . . .

When I graduated from Howard University, I was still up under that "Babylonian" weight, so I looked around to see who was watching me, and I said a cool, "Thank you, Jesus." When they gave me my master's degree, I was a little higher up and felt a little more free, so I said a little louder, "Thank you, Jesus." People were looking at me. Then, when it was time for my doctorate, the president of the university was there; the chancellor was there. They put the diploma in my hand and said, "All the rights and privileges there unto appertaining," and I said, "Thank you, Jesus!" The higher up you go, the louder you're supposed to holler. Don't let go of your faith, even in a foreign land.

If you want to know how to hold on, no matter what, just remember the story of my daddy. My daddy used to be an embarrassment to me until I found out a few things. He came straight off the farm. His father sent him to college with twenty-five cents, and Daddy had twelve earned letters behind his name: a B.Th., a B.A., an M.Div., and an

S.T.M. He had four degrees: one undergraduate, two graduate from Virginia Union University, a black school, and one
from the Lutheran School of Theology. Like Martin Luther
King, my daddy's mind had been honed by the finest schol-
arship in German theological circles. Like Daniel, my daddy
knew "Babylonian" theology, christology, homiletics, and
hermeneutics. He had studied "Babylonian" exegesis and
mastered form criticism.[23]

My daddy had gone all the way up the ladder, but where
the "Babylonians" had honed his mind, the God of Abraham
and Sarah had tuned his heart. When he came home from
his ministerial association meeting one cold Monday afternoon in September of 1941, they told him that his wife, who
had had a difficult pregnancy, had passed out on the floor.
The baby had come out six months into her pregnancy with
the umbilical cord wrapped around its neck. At the hospital
the baby had been pronounced dead on arrival, and they
were trying to save his wife. My daddy didn't call on no
"Babylonian" theology; my daddy didn't look up no "Babylonian" christology; my daddy got down on his knees right
there on the floor next to his wife's blood and called on the
God of Abraham and Sarah, Isaac and Rebekah, and said,
"Lord, if you can and if you will, I know you can save my
boy." And fifty-two years later, here is the one that was pronounced dead on arrival. Don't you tell me what God can't
do. God stepped into that emergency room. While my father
was just praying, the Lord stepped in and changed the diag-
nosis from dead on arrival to divinity on the agenda.

Thank God! Thank God! Don't let go of your faith. I
don't care how high up you go. Don't let go of your faith.

Study Questions

1. How does Psalm 137:4 (GNB) – "How can we sing a
song to the LORD in a foreign land?" – capture the difficul-

ties that persons encounter when they are forced to leave their homelands?

2. In what ways does this sermon compare the Jews' exile experience in Babylon to African Americans' exile experiences in the United States?

3. The last paragraph in the sermon's introduction, beginning with Pythagorean mathematics and ending with Islam, points out that the foundations of the world's knowledge and religions were laid by African people. Look at one or more of these branches of knowledge and religion and tell how it is a foundation for what we know and practice today.

4. According to ideas in this sermon, what's in a name? What does your surname tell about your family's history?

5. Alex Haley's Kunte Kinte (Roots) strongly resisted being called "Toby" by his slave master. How is the story of his resistance a miniature lesson in history about forced assimilation and the problems that it brings?

6. What can be done to make our school curricula more multicultural, particularly in teaching history and literature? Is it conceivable that some Eurocentric history and literature could be abridged or left out in order to include the major works of other cultures that make up the North American landscape?

7. What does the poem "I Am an African" tell you about so-called savage or primitive African beliefs?

8. In what ways have African Americans in this foreign land maintained their faith?

9. After being in the United States for hundreds of years, are African Americans still in a "foreign land," or can they

sing, along with the other immigrants to this country, about this land being their land, one made for all people?

10. Have you or anyone you have known shed your lively inherited African expressions of the faith in favor of more sophisticated and quiet forms of worship and praise? Was it right or wrong to do this? expedient? political? proper? in good taste? biblical? pleasing to God? Was it of no consequence as long as you acknowledged God? Do you believe that "the higher up you go the louder you ought to holler"?

What Makes You So Strong?

Judges 16:4-31

What makes you so strong, black man? How is it that 370 years of slavery, segregation, racism, Jim Crow laws, and second-class citizenship cannot wipe out the memory of Imhotep, Aesop, Akhenaton, and Thutmose II?[1] What makes you so strong, black man?

How is it that after all this country has done to you, you can still produce a Paul Robeson, a Thurgood Marshall, a Malcolm X (el-Hajj Malik el-Shabazz), a Martin King, and a Ron McNair?[2] What makes you so strong, black man?

This country has tried castration and lynching, miseducation and brainwashing. They have taught you to hate yourself and to look at yourself through the awfully tainted eyeglasses of white Eurocentric lies, and yet you keep breaking out of the prisons they put you in. You break out in a W.E.B. Dubois and a Booker T. Washington;[3] you break out in a Louis Farrakhan and a Mickey Leland;[4] you break out in a Judge Thurgood Marshall and a Pops Staples;[5] you break out in a Luther Vandross, Magic Johnson, Michael Jordan, Harold Washington, or a Doug Wilder.[6] What makes you so strong, black man?

I don't care what field we pick, you produce a giant in that field. What makes you so strong? The world tried the poisons of self-hatred, of distorted history, of false standards of beauty. They taught you that you were ugly and stupid, slow and retarded, dimwitted and dull-witted, good only for stud service and getting high, and yet you keep on

turning out a Sterling Brown and Vincent Harding, a Jim
Forbes and Kwame Nkrumah, an Allan Boesak and William
Gray, a Steve Biko and Bill Cosby, a Dave Dinkins and Doug
Wilder.[7] What makes you so strong, black man?

And speaking of Sterling Brown, he wrote about you
when he said "the strong men keep coming on."[8] He wrote:

> They dragged you from your homeland,
> They chained you in coffles,
> They huddled you spoon-fashion in filthy hatches,
> They sold you to give a few gentlemen ease.
>
> They broke you in like oxen,
> They scourged you,
> They branded you,
> They made your women breeders,
> They swelled your numbers with bastards...
> They taught you the religion they disgraced.
>
> You sang:
>   Keep a-inchin' along
>   Lak a po' inch worm...
>
> You sang:
>   Bye and bye
>   I'm gonna lay down dis heaby load...
>
> You sang:
>   Walk togedder, chillen,
>   Dontcha git weary...
>   *The strong men keep a-comin' on*
>   *The strong men git stronger.*
>
> They point with pride to the roads you built for them.
> They ride in comfort over the rails you laid for them.
> They put hammers in your hands
> And said—Drive so much before sundown.
>
> You sang:
>   Ain't no hammah
>   In dis lan',
>   Strikes lak mine, bebby,
>   Strikes lak mine.

They cooped you in their kitchens,
They penned you in their factories,
They gave you the jobs that they were too good for,
They tried to guarantee happiness to themselves
By shunting dirt and misery to you.

You sang:
    Me an' muh baby gonna shine, shine
    Me an' muh baby gonna shine.
      The strong men keep a-comin' on
      The strong men git stronger...

They bought off some of your leaders
You stumbled, as blind men will...
They coaxed you, unwontedly soft-voiced...
You followed a way.
Then laughed as usual.

They heard the laugh and wondered;
Uncomfortable;
Unadmitting a deeper terror...
    The strong men keep a-comin' on
    Gittin' stronger...

What, from the slums
Where they have hemmed you,
What, from the tiny huts
They could not keep from you—
What reaches them
Making them ill at ease, fearful?
Today they shout prohibition at you
"Thou shalt not this"
"Thou shalt not that"
"Reserved for whites only"
You laugh.

One thing they cannot prohibit—
    The strong men...coming on
    The strong men gittin' stronger.
    Strong men...
    STRONGER...

What makes you so strong, black man? And what makes
you so strong, black woman? How could you produce a

Queen Hatshepset[9] whose reign was one of the most outstanding in the Eighteenth Dynasty of Egypt. This African
queen ruled powerfully, masterfully, and with dignity fifteen
hundred years before our Lord Jesus Christ was born. How
could you produce the warrior queens of Ethiopia and Nubia and the five fine queens known as Candace[10] who opposed the southward movement of the armies of Alexander
the Great and changed the whole course of Greek history?
What makes you so strong, black woman?

How is it that 370 years of being used as a breeder and a
toy for the master, and being used as a punching bag for
Willie Lee, and being messed on and messed over, walked on
and walked out on – how is it that 370 years of that does not
kill the spirit of Queen Ann Nzinga; Cleopatra; Nefertiti;
Makeda, the Queen of Sheba; Mary, the mother of Jesus;
and Hadassah,[11] the rebel queen who defiantly said, "If I
perish, I perish"? What makes you so strong, black woman?

How is it that after all this world has done to you, after
all white women have done to you, after all white men have
done to you, after all black men have done to you, you can
still produce an Angela Davis, a Toni Morrison, a Barbara
Jordan, a Betty Shabazz, an Oprah Winfrey, and a Winnie
Mandela.[12] What makes you so strong, black woman?

This country has tried negation and degradation. They
have taught you to look down on your broad hips and thick
lips. They've taught you to hate your hair and to keep it at
all costs from going back. Going back to what? Africa? Going back to the way God made it? to what? They have
taught you that the less you look like "Miss Ann," the worse
off you are. And yet you keep breaking out of the prisons
they put you in. You break out in a Nannie Burroughs, a
Fannie Lou Hamer, and a Jessie "Ma" Houston.[13] You break
out in a Roberta Flack, an Anita Baker, a Jackie Joyner-
Kersee and a Nina Simone.[14] I don't care what field we pick,
you black women keep turning out giants in the field, even
those fields they told you were reserved for men only. What
makes you so strong, black woman?

They told you that you were not allowed in the field of
medicine, and here you come with a black M.D. graduating

from medical school in the 1800s.[15] What makes you so strong, black woman? They told you that no black women were allowed in the field of ministry, and here you come with the Reverends Jini Moore, Gwenn Pierre, Barbara Williams, Lola Nelson, Devanah Johns, Lana Reese, LaVerne Harris, Mickey Moseley, the Reverend Joan Campbell, and Bishop Barbara Harris.[16] What makes you so strong, black woman? They told you no women were allowed in the male-dominated field of TV journalism, and here you come with a Melanie Lawson[17] and an Oprah Winfrey. They tried the poison of low self-esteem; they tried the poison of low expectations; they tried the poison of lesbianism; they tried the poison of despair. They told you the numbers aren't there—the brothers are in prison, on dope, unemployed. And what do you do? You refuse to give up. You keep on turning out Zora Neal Hurstons and Mari Evanses, Mary Se Condes and Gladys Knights.[18] You keep on turning out Winnie Mandelas and the mothers of Zimbabwe, the mothers of Soweto, the mothers of Angola, the mothers of Namibia,[19] the mothers of Mississippi. What makes you so strong, black woman?

What makes you so strong, black people? No other race was brought to this country in chains. No other race had laws passed making it a crime to teach them how to read. No other race had skin color as the determining factor of their servitude and their employability. No other race was hounded and haunted when they wanted to be free. No other race was physically mutilated to identify them as property, not people. No other race was lied to and lied on like the African race. No other race had its names taken away in addition to its language and music. No other race was denied more and deprived of more, treated as badly and treated as less than human. No other race was treated like the Africans were treated, and yet no other race has done so much after starting out with so little, defying all of the odds and breaking all of the records. What makes you so strong, black people? How were you able to do that? Jimmy the Greek wants to know. Tom Brokaw wants to know. Ted Koppel wants to know. Geraldo wants to know. I have a feeling that Oprah Winfrey already knows. What makes you so strong, black people?

How were you able to build the great pyramids of Cheops?[20] How were you able to build the grand lodge of Maat? How were you able to build the first universities in the world? How were you able to survive the horrors of slavery, to survive the loss of two hundred million in the Atlantic Ocean, to survive the hatred of Europeans, to survive a holocaust five times worse than Hitler's holocaust, and to then take a Jesse Owens over on Hitler's turf and stick it in Hitler's ear?[21] How were you able to do that? What makes you so strong, black people? Is it something in your African blood? Is it something in your African psyche? Is it something in your African soul? Is it something in your African spirit? What makes you so strong, black people?

Samson's Weakness

How is it that you keep coming? You see, that was Delilah's question. And one of Samson's problems was that he answered her question. If you read this whole biography of Samson, you discover that Samson had several problems. He never did get that love thing straight. Samson was reared in a God-fearing home. His mother and father were together. He had a strong male role model, but he never could pull off that right combination in terms of a committed relationship. Dr. Jawanza Kunjufu[22] of our church would say that his focus was on the outside, the external, and not on the inside, the internal.

Samson ruled Israel for twenty years, and he ruled during some tough times. His people were under oppression. His people were constantly under attack. They were assaulted by the twin demons of assimilation and segregation. Though Samson ruled successfully for twenty years politically, he never was quite able to put it all together in his personal life. He kept being attracted to girls of another race. (It's in the book.) And he kept acting on those attractions as if they were love. First, he had his mother and daddy set up a marriage with somebody he didn't even know. Why would you do that Samson? "Cause she looked good and makes me feel good." Then he tried sex without commitment. He went to bed with a prostitute.

He was able to judge disputes between conflicting parties; he was able to judge lawsuits – civil suits and criminal suits. He was able to administer the office of judge with prudence and integrity. He had twenty years of service on the bench with no bribes, no deals, no tarnish on his integrity. He was a judge of Israel for two decades in an oppressive and hostile situation. He judged a people who sometimes turned *on* each other rather than turning *to* each other. He judged a people whom sociologists would say were a permanent underclass, with no chance for survival or success. He was brilliant in his political life, but he bombed out in his personal life. He was absolutely no judge of character and a complete failure when it came to judging the opposite sex or choosing relationships with them.

After a marriage that did not work out and after a hooker who set him up, he saw another fine woman with a body by Fisher, and he was hooked. Everyone has got a certain weakness in life. Well, good looks and good sex just happened to be Samson's weaknesses. Not once does the Scripture say that Delilah cared anything at all about him. She had men waiting in another room. But he didn't care; he loved her. She looked good and she made him feel good – a transient reality. Not only did she not feel the same way, she made it plain that money meant more to her than a man. But even after she tricked him three times, Samson kept right on going back. Love wouldn't let him wait, and love wouldn't let him think. Then again, Samson did not know the difference between love and lust, between looking good and feeling good. You see, love is internal; looks and lust are external.

Contract or Covenant

Samson had some problems, but his biggest problem was that he answered Delilah's question. He told somebody who didn't care anything about him, and who had made that obvious, that which was of ultimate importance in his life. The King James Version of that passage says, "he told her all his heart" (Judges 16:17). The Hebrew word is *leb*, connoting feeling, will, intellect, the center of everything. Dr. John Kinney, Dean and Associate Professor of Theological Studies at Virginia Union School of Theology said, "Can't nobody but God keep your whole heart. You don't give your whole heart to nobody but God." And Kinney was just echoing what Jesus said: "Thou shalt love the Lord thy God with all thy heart" (Matthew 22:36, KJV).

You see, nobody can keep your heart like God can. Oh, a person can tug at your heart strings and make your heart heavy or happy. A person can hurt your heart or break your heart. He can make your heart skip a beat; she can make your heart glad or sad, but nobody can keep your whole heart. Nobody can handle it. Only God has hands big enough to handle your whole heart.

What makes you so strong, Samson? How can you say you love me if you won't tell me what makes you so strong? How can you say you love me if you won't go to bed with me? How can you say you love me if you won't try this cocaine with me? How can you say you love me if you won't buy this thing for me? How can you say you love me if you won't do like I ask? Watch those *if* clauses. If you get an *if* clause in the relationship, that's a contract, and love isn't a contract; love is a covenant.

Dr. Jawanza Kunjufu said his grandmama put it this way: "I make sure I give 110 percent every day. It ain't about what he gives; I got to make sure I give all I got every day." You see, that's a covenant. It's not *if . . . then;* it's *nevertheless, in spite of, anyhow*. There's a book called *The Dance-Away Lover*[23] that talks about the three stages in relationships. There is the romance stage in all relationships, and we like that. There's the problem stage; then there's the commitment stage. To reach the commitment stage, you have to move from romance through problems, down to commitment. But what do we do? We enjoy the romance stage, and then as soon as we run into problems we dance away and find ourselves another lover.

A covenant is moving past romance through the problems. That's commitment. I'm committed *nevertheless*; I'm committed *in spite of*; I'm committed *anyhow*. I'm not going anywhere because I'm going to have problems everywhere. Why? Because I'm going there and I'm taking some problems with me. That's commitment and covenant.

Second, that same person who lights up your life and starts the juices flowing is the one who is going to get on your last nerve. The same person does both. Samson didn't know that. He was only a good judge of matters of the head. He didn't know too much about matters of the heart. Maybe his Nazirite[24] vow kept him from nurturing those relationships that would have taught him about the heart. So when Delilah pulled that *if . . . then* trick on him, she had him. How can you say you love me if you won't tell me what makes you so strong? She vexed him, the King James Version says, until he told her his whole heart, that which was of ultimate importance in life. He told her what my mama used to call the God's honest truth!

Guard God's Will for Your Life

Samson revealed his secret to his enemy (to this one who cared nothing about him). He told her about his special relationship with God. He allowed his desire for her to take precedence over his devotion to God. Watch out! Don't let what somebody can do *to* you or do *for* you become more important than what God wants to do *in* you and *through* you. You see, God had set the terms for Samson's life and his labors long before Samson was born. God had set up the relationship between his servant and himself before Samson drew his first breath. God had a work to do in and through Samson. That's why he sent the angel to announce what he had on his mind.[25]

You see, God has a work that he wants to do through African Americans – a people who have known hatred, yet who still have the strength to love; a people who have known degradation, yet who still have the strength to stand tall and produce giant after giant in field after field; a people who have known belittlement and humiliation, yet who have maintained their integrity and kept their souls intact; a people who have been lied to, lied on, and lied about, yet who still have the strength to forgive and to build strong families, regardless of those families' configuration. God has a work of redemption and healing to do through African Americans. God will do through you individually, not only corporately. Don't you know that God only made one of you, and that God pulled off a miracle when he put you together and then threw away the pattern? Watch out for what somebody can do *to* you and *for* you. Don't let that become more important than what our God wants to do *in* you and *through* you. Samson allowed a relationship that he wanted to have but could not have get in the way of the relationship that he already had with God.

They'll Put You in Chains

Samson revealed his secret to his enemy; he told Delilah about his relationship with God. Then he shared with her that which symbolized his special relationship with God. See what happens when you reveal your whole heart to others? First, they put you in chains. You give them your heart; they chain your body and then your mind. As Dr. Carter G. Woodson and Dr. Bobby Wright[26] would both say: They can take the chains off your bodies and have absolutely nothing to fear from your mind.

Dr. Woodson said it this way: "If you tell a person to go to the back door over and over again, then one day you say, 'You no longer have to go to the back door,' do you know what that person will do? He will not only go to the back door, but if there is not one back there, he'll cut one in."

Bobby Wright was a little more earthy in saying it this way: "If they can put the chains on your mind, your behind will follow." They can chain your mind and have nothing to fear from your body. They put you in chains philosophically and psychologically. They tell you, "You ain't nothing. You ain't done nothing. Your daddy before you wasn't nothing, and your mama ain't nothing. You ain't come from nothing; you got nothing to offer, and you ain't never gonna amount to nothing."

They'll trap you in vocational training, half teaching you a skill that you can never use. They'll put you in chains sociologically, giving you the poorest schools and the worst equipment. They'll give you the worst housing at the highest cost. You'll get the lowest paying jobs, but the most whiskey, drugs, and guns so you can kill each other and save them the trouble.

They'll put you in chains theologically and have you worship their god, *Dagon*.[27] Only we don't call him Dagon anymore; we call him "Dough-sky" (Prosperity). "All that God has you can get. Come on. Just send me five dollars and I'll send you a blessed cloth. You can have it! You can have it!" They'll put you in chains theologically and have you worshiping an alien theology.

They'll Blind You

Keep reading this passage. They'll put your eyes out so you can't even see what's happening to you. You can't see the psychological chains, the physiological chains, the economic chains, the educational chains, the sociological chains, or even the drug addiction chains they've put you through. Do you know what happens when you can't see? You, the victims, become the staunchest supporters of a sick system of perpetual slavery because you can't see what the enemy has done and keeps on doing to you. Sterling Brown wrote about that half a century ago when he said, "they bought off some of your leaders, and you stumbled as blind men will."

They put chains on you. They put your eyes out. Then look at verses 24 and 25. They led Samson out and paraded him in front of the nation to make fun of him. They'll parade you on television documentaries and news shows. They'll parade you as the primary example of pathology in America. They'll parade you as the user and the victim of the drugs that they brought into the country in the first place. Why is it that with a drug czar and the millions of dollars that we spend to fight drugs, we can't stop drugs from coming into the country? But they parade you as the primary victims. They shout, "Bring him out. Let him entertain us. You know his kind always make the best entertainers."

They made fun of Samson because of what they had done

to him. They made fun of him because he used to be so strong, and now, because of his desire for one of their women, he was reduced to a nothing and a nobody. You think that's only in the Bible? Look at what they did to Senator Brooke.[28] They made fun of Samson because he couldn't see where he was, couldn't see what was happening to him, and couldn't see where he was going. He had to be led around by a little boy. It might be that the little black children will be the ones to get us blind old folks out of this mess we've gotten ourselves into. They made fun of Samson because they had in chains the one who used to whip them. He was a part of their prison system, and they weren't about to let him go. "Call Samson out and make him entertain us!"

The Symbol Is Not the Source

But the thing that Delilah missed, and that his enemy missed, was the whole answer to what made him so strong. You see, they mistook the symbol of his strength for the source of his strength. They didn't listen to his whole answer. His hair was the symbol, not the source. Look at his whole answer. He said, "My hair has never been cut." That's a symbol. Why? "Because I have been dedicated to God as a Nazirite from the time I was born." Now that's the source of his strength. The last verse of chapter 13 says, "The LORD's power began to strengthen him."[29] But the Hebrew says the *ruah*, the Spirit of the Lord, began to move him.

In chapter 14, when a lion attacked (v. 6), it says again the *ruah*, the Spirit of the Lord, came upon him. In chapter 15, when he grabbed that jawbone of an ass, verse 14 says the *ruah*, the Spirit of the Lord, came mightily upon him. The source of his strength was God, and the *ruah*, the Spirit of God. So he prayed (16:28) after his hair, the symbol of strength, began to grow back, "Lord, try me one more time. I know I let you down before, but try me just one more time. Give me my strength just this one more time." What he's asking for is God's Spirit, the *ruah*, God's strength, not his own.

What makes us so strong? God's strength. David answered the question: "God is our refuge and strength."[30] What makes us so strong? Isaiah answered the question: "He giveth power to the faint; and to them that have no might he increaseth strength."[31] God is the source of our strength.

What makes us so strong? The same thing that empowered Martin King. Not the school in Boston, but God's Spirit; not what he learned at Crozer, but God's Spirit; not what he learned in seminary, but God's Spirit.[32] Martin was the man he was because of the Spirit of God.

What makes us so strong? God is the joy and strength of my life. When I don't have any strength, I call on him who is my strength. When I can't make it on my own, I call on the one who can make a way out of no way. *Father, I stretch my hands to thee. No other help I know. If thou withdraw thyself from me, whither shall I go?*

The Lord is my strength and my salvation. This applies to preachers, too. People have their preferences when it comes to preachers. Some people like preachers with manuscripts; others like preachers without manuscripts. Some like preachers who can "tune" a little while, and all of that kind of stuff. But let me tell you something: this preaching business isn't as easy as it looks. Sometimes I don't feel like preaching. Sometimes my spirit is too impoverished to preach. I've been in some churches in this country where the folk are so cold they kill my spirit. Sometimes they do it with the music.[33] And so I've had, on occasion, to disrupt a service. Once I stood up in a prestigious university chapel and began to spontaneously sing the way my grandmama used to sing, "Guide my feet, Lord, while I run this race, 'cause I don't want to run this race in vain." Folks started looking at their programs trying to figure out where this came in. While I was singing my grandmama's song, I could feel my grandmama's spirit (she used to sing that song while she rocked me on her knee) getting all into my spirit. I could feel her hooking up with the Holy Ghost and passing him down to me.

Our strength comes from the Spirit of God. This same Spirit of God will empower you as he empowered our Lord,

Jesus Christ. Jesus promised that he would give the Spirit to you. He has never failed on any of his promises. This is what makes us so strong.

Study Questions

1. Look at the situations that Sterling Brown describes and the songs that he quotes in his poem "The Strong Men." Look at each song. What message is in each one?

2. Choose at least one Egyptian and at least one African American strong man that was mentioned. Examine their lives and list their strengths.

3. Choose at least one of the African queens and at least one African American woman that Dr. Wright mentions. Examine their lives and list their strengths.

4. To what does the African holocaust refer? How is the strength of African Americans magnified in light of so great a historical atrocity?

5. Samson was a "womanizer." Samson's weakness for the opposite sex is not unknown to the African American community. Both men and women have been afflicted, all too often having sought their personal value or sense of self in meaningless alliances with the opposite sex. How can we begin to reverse this trend?

6. Look at Delilah's actions. She represents a person who is willing to relate to somebody solely for personal gain. Her approach to Samson is, "What can you do for me?" Give examples of male-female relationships today that are based on this approach.

7. God has a purpose for each person's life, as he had a purpose for Samson's. Discovering the purpose is only step

one in realizing it. There are always people, forces, and situations that can deter one from his or her purpose. These deterrents can be very subtle. What are some of them?

8. How can we successfully guard God's purpose or will for our lives?

9. Samson was subdued, chained, and blinded. He was no longer able to do the things God had willed for him to do. Look at today's society's chains and blinders that are enumerated. How can we begin to break these chains and remove these blinders?

10. What makes you so strong? Share your favorite Scripture and/or a testimony.

FOOTNOTES

Unexpected Blessings
[1] Matthew 18:20, RSV
[2] John 7:46, RSV
[3] James 4:7, RSV
[4] Matthew 16:18, KJV
[5] Mark 14:66-72; Matthew 26:69-75; Luke 22:1-62
[6] Dr. Charles Walker is the pastor of the Nineteenth Street Baptist Church in Philadelphia.
[7] Isaiah 40:31, KJV
[8] Traditional

Ain't Nobody Right but Us
[1] Dr. James Forbes is the former Brown-Sockman Professor of Homiletics at Union Theological Seminary in New York City, and presently the pastor of Riverside Church there.
[2] Janice Hale Benson. *Black Children: Their Roots, Culture and Learning Styles.* Salt Lake City: Brigham Young University Press, 1982.
[3] A diphthong is a single sound within one syllable that has two parts, such as the oy in boy. It begins with the tongue in one position for the o and in another position for the "ee" sound (y).
[4] Geneva Smitherman. *Talkin' and Testifyin': The Language of Black Americans.* Detroit: Wayne State University Press, 1989.
[5] Linguists learned this by observing Jews in Nazi German concentration camps.
[6] M.C. Hammer is a popular and positive musical rap artist who has popularized a particular style of dancing, which bears his name.

⁷ M.C. Hammer, "U Can't Touch This," *Here Comes the Hammer* album, 1990-91.
⁸ Lamentations 3:22-23, KJV.

Unhitch the Trailer
¹ Miriam and Aaron, Moses' sister and brother, spoke against his marriage to a Cushite (Ethiopian) woman.
² The Casbah at Cairo is its citadel, or fortress.
³ Genesis 28:10-22
⁴ Joel 2:28-29; Acts 2:17, KJV
⁵ Romans 8:28, NRSV
⁶ Genesis 18:14, RSV
⁷ Philippians 4:13, NRSV
⁸ Proverbs 23:7, KJV
⁹ Isaiah 26:3, RSV
¹⁰ PRN means as needed. TID means take three times a day.
¹¹ Philippians 4:6-7, NRSV
¹² Philippians 4:8-9, NRSV
¹³ Philippians 3:13-14, NRSV
¹⁴ *The Little Engine That Could*, by Watty Piper
¹⁵ Acts 13:13
¹⁶ Acts 15:37-40
¹⁷ 2 Timothy 4:10

What's in This for Me?
¹ The Diaspora first referred to the scattered Jews living outside of Palestine after the Babylonian Exile. The word is derived from the Greek *diaspeirein* which means "to scatter." Scholars of African descent have applied the term to African peoples who have been scattered throughout the world as a result of centuries of slave trading.
² Carter G. Woodson (1875-1950) was an African American historian who is credited with initiating Black Studies as an academic field in schools and colleges. In 1926 he founded Negro History Week, now Black History Month, which is observed in February each year.
³ The "I am" sayings of Jesus are found in the Gospel of John. See John 6:35 (bread of Life); 10:11 (good shepherd); 14:6 (way, truth, life).
⁴ Matthew 17:1-13; Mark 9:2-8; Luke 9:28-36; 2 Peter 1:16-21.
⁵ Peter's denial of Jesus is recorded in Matthew 26:69-75; Mark 14:66-72; Luke 22:54-62; and John 18:15-18, 25-27.
⁶ Charles Walker is the pastor of the Nineteenth Street Baptist Church in Philadelphia. Also a musician, he was the former minister of music for the Reverend Clay Evans in Chicago. He served as accompanist for Mahalia Jackson and wrote *Requiem for Martin*, the piece performed by the Boston Sym-

phony Orchestra in honor of Dr. Martin Luther King's life and
death. Bill Jones is pastor of Bethany Baptist Church in
Brooklyn, New York, and author of *God in the Ghetto*.
7 The Kemetic religion is an ancient Egyptian religion, empha-
sizing truth, enlightenment, and education, as well as aspects
of eschatology, cosmology, morals, and ethics.
8 Dr. Jacob Carruthers is author of *Essays in Ancient Egyptian Studies*.
9 "Conscious" is the term used for nationalists who are Afrocen-
tric in perspective.
10 "Some Day," by C.A. Tindley.

When You Forget Who You Are
1 Genesis 18:14
2 Genesis 22:13
3 Genesis 37:28
4 Genesis 50:20
5 Exodus 14:21
6 Joshua 10:13
7 2 Kings 2:11
8 Daniel 6:22
9 Daniel 3:25-26
10 Jeremiah 20:9
11 Esther 2:7, 17
12 Esther 2:1-4
13 Maroons were fugitive African slaves.
14 A courageous group of slaves aboard the slave ship *Amistad*
mutinied in the mid-nineteenth century, escaping from their
Spanish owners off the coast of Cuba. They brought the *Amistad* into the United States, near Long Island. They were de-
fended before the Supreme Court in 1841 by John Quincy
Adams. Adams' successful defense gained their freedom and
prevented their return to their owners, which would have
brought on punishment by death.
15 This program aired in 1979, with James Earl Jones as the
narrator.
16 Vuitton and Coach are popular labels in clothing and leather
accessories.
17 The Diaspora first referred to the scattered Jews living outside of Palestine after the Babylonian Exile. The word is derived from the Greek *diaspeirein* which means "to scatter."
Scholars of African descent have applied the term to African
peoples who have been scattered throughout the world as a
result of centuries of slave trading.
18 United Church of Christ
19 The Reverend James Forbes is currently the pastor, and the

first African American pastor, of the renowned Riverside Church in New York City.
[20] Carlyle Marney (1916–1978) was a Baptist minister who pastored in churches in Texas and North Carolina from the 1940s to the 1960s. He founded Interpreter's House, an ecumenical center in North Carolina, and was its director for many years. He taught at several colleges, including Southern Methodist University, and was a visiting professor at the Divinity School at Duke University in 1972. He is the author of several books, including *Faith in Conflict, The Carpenter's Son, A Recovery of the Person: A Christian Humanism*, and *The Crucible of Redemption*.

Full of the Holy Spirit
[1] John J. Ansbro. *Martin Luther King, Jr.: The Making of a Mind*. Maryknoll, N.Y.: Orbis Books, 1984.
[2] Dr. King earned the Ph.D. degree at Boston University in 1955.
[3] Dr. King attended Morehouse College in Atlanta, where Dr. Benjamin E. Mays served as president from 1940 to 1967.
[4] Dr. James H. Cone is the Briggs Distinguished Professor at Union Theological Seminary in New York, and is the author and coauthor of several books that shaped black theology. He also is author of *Martin and Malcolm and America: A Dream or a Nightmare* (Orbis).
[5] A Puritan-influenced Christian belief is that secular music has no place in the life of the Christian, and especially not in the preacher's life. This is an allusion to a question by someone who heard me refer to jazz trumpeter Wynton Marsalis, and who did not understand why I would be familiar with or appreciative of jazz music. (I am on one of Wynton Marsalis's albums!) The irony in this belief about secular music is that it has seldom applied to European-influenced "classical" music, which also is secular, so the belief is scandalously tainted by the all-too-familiar double standard of racism.
[6] The A.M.E. Church is the African Methodist Episcopal Church.
[7] John 4:7-30
[8] Deuteronomy 5:4; 34:10
[9] Psalm 51:10-12, KJV
[10] Judges 4-5
[11] Ruth 1:16, KJV
[12] 1 Kings 18:44-45
[13] 1 Kings 18:17-40
[14] 2 Kings 2:11
[15] Isaiah 6:1

16 Isaiah 9:6, KJV
17 Isaiah 40:4-5, KJV
18 Isaiah 53:5, KJV
19 Isaiah 40:28-31, KJV
20 The Proctor Programs are Doctor of Ministry programs at United Theological Seminary in Dayton, Ohio. Of the several Doctor of Ministry programs, two are named in part for Dr. Samuel DeWitt Proctor, former pastor of the Abyssinian Baptist Church in Harlem.
21 Abyssinian Baptist Church in the heart of New York City's Harlem was founded in 1808, making it the oldest black Baptist church in New York City. Dr. Proctor served as one of the distinguished pastors of the church, which became well known nationally during the pastorate of Congressman Adam Clayton Powell.
22 Minister Louis Farrakhan is the leader of the Nation of Islam, which was developed by the Honorable Elijah Muhammad.
23 A. Lewis Patterson is the pastor of Mount Corinth Baptist Church in Houston, Texas.
24 John 8:44
25 Philippians 4:13, NRSV
26 Romans 8:31, RSV
27 The hymn "God Will Take Care of You" was written by Civilla D. Martin.
28 See previous footnote.

The Audacity to Hope

1 The Sharpeville Massacre occurred on March 21, 1960, in the black township of Sharpeville, a suburb of Vereeniging. Some twenty thousand Africans gathered at a police station in Sharpeville for a demonstration against pass laws, organized by the Pan Africanist Congress. South African blacks were required to carry passes with them at all times and to produce them upon demand by police officers and other officials. The scene that day at Sharpeville turned bloody when the police opened fire on the crowd with submachine guns. Sixty-seven Africans were killed, and 186 were wounded. Among the victims were forty-eight women and children. This incident helped to focus international attention on South Africa's cruel system of apartheid.
2 "Reefer," a term that has been replaced by "weed" and other slang words, refers to marijuana.
3 The Reverend J. H. Jackson was head of the National Baptist Convention. He expelled Dr. King and other civil rights activists from the convention during the 1960s because he thought

their approach to civil rights was too militant. For an account of Chicago Mayor Richard Daley's treatment of Dr. King and the members of the Southern Christian Leadership Conference during their campaign in Chicago, see the chapter "Chicago" in *And the Walls Came Tumbling Down*, by Ralph David Abernathy (New York: Harper Perennial, 1990).

[4] Romans 5:3-4
[5] Also see James 1:2-4
[6] Romans 5:5, KJV
[7] Romans 8:24-25, author's paraphrase
[8] Isaiah 40:31, RSV
[9] Traditional
[10] Traditional
[11] Traditional
[12] This is an Arabic benediction used by the Islamic religion which means "Peace be unto you."

When God Is Silent

[1] Psalm 27:5, KJV
[2] Revelation 1:13-15
[3] Song of Solomon 1:5, author's paraphrase
[4] Traditional song of the black church
[5] Aunt Hannah's children is an old light-hearted term used by African Americans to refer to one another when they are "acting out" or being nuisances or bothersome in irritating but not necessarily malicious ways.
[6] Psalm 121:1, KJV
[7] Job 37:9, GNB
[8] Job 24:12, GNB
[9] Job 23:3, RSV
[10] 1 Kings 19:4, GNB
[11] Matthew 27:46, RSV
[12] Throughout the Book of Job, his friends Bildad, Eliphaz, Zophar, and the young Elihu try to convince him that he would not be experiencing such excruciating suffering if he had not done something very wrong.
[13] 1 Kings 19:2, author's paraphrase
[14] Luke 23:5-39, author's paraphrase
[15] Isaiah 55:8-9
[16] 1 Kings 19:11-12
[17] Habakkuk 2:20, RSV
[18] 2 Corinthians 5:7
[19] 1 John 3:2, KJV
[20] 1 Kings 19:18
[21] Hebrews 11:1, NRSV
[22] A.M.E. stands for the African Methodist Episcopal Church.
[23] The story of Faust, who sold his soul to the devil, was written

by English dramatist Christopher Marlowe (*Dr. Faustus*, 1604). Mephistopheles, also called Mephisto, was the name given to the spirit of the devil in the Faust legend.
[24] Dexter C. Wise III formerly pastored the Shiloh Baptist Church in Columbus, Ohio. Wyatt Tee Walker is the pastor of Canaan Baptist Church in New York City and author of several books relating to the African American religious experience. One of his most recent books is *Spirits That Dwell in Deep Woods III* (New York: Martin Luther King Fellows Press, 1991).

Faith in a Foreign Land
[1] Psalm 137:1-4, GNB
[2] Hand jive and hambone, games enjoyed by African American children, employ rhythmic chants, claps, and body-slapping motions with the hand from thigh to shoulder.

> Hambone, hambone have you heard?
> (slap slap slap-slap, slap slap)
> Papa's gonna buy us a mockingbird.
> (slap slap slap-slap, slap slap)

[3] Similar to hand jive, Double-Dutch is a rhythmic rope jumping game in which two crisscrossing ropes are turned on a beat by two turners standing opposite each other, while a jumper jumps in the midst of the two ropes and performs a dance-like routine, skillfully stepping in order to avoid being tripped by either rope.
[4] Pythagorean mathematics is so named for the Greek philosopher Pythagoras. The Pythagorean theorem is a formula used to find the length of the sides of a triangle.
[5] Thales of Miletus, the Ionian philosopher-scientist of the sixth and seventh centuries, was credited with initiating the theory of the four elements by declaring that water was a central principle or element of his cosmology. It is said that his successors then defined the other primary elements as fire, earth, and air.
[6] Epicurean materialism was the thought of Epicurus, a first-century Roman philosopher, who taught that atoms conform to an up-down direction in space and therefore fall in parallel paths. To explain their impact upon one another, he said that atoms were subject to chance swerves. This doctrine was also used to explain free will.
[7] Plato was the second of the trio of great ancient Greek philosophers (Socrates, Plato, Aristotle). He lived in the third and fourth centuries before Christ and taught that absolute values are rooted in unchanging and eternal realities that are independent of what we can perceive through our five senses.
[8] Luke 1:5-24

[9] Not only were the meaningful names of the Hebrew boys changed, but the Babylonian names that they were given were idolatrous. Daniel's name included the "El," meaning "God." His name meant "God is my judge." The Babylonian name for their god was "Bel," so his new name, "Belteshazzar," meant "May Bel protect his life." Every time this name was said, God was profaned. Similarly, Hananiah, meaning "Yahweh is gracious," was changed to Shadrach, which meant "command of Aku," the moon god. Mishael again contained "El," the Hebrew name for God. It meant "Who is what God is?" But Meshach is believed to have meant "Who is what Aku is?" Azariah meant "Whom Yahweh helps." His Babylonian name, Abednego, meant "Servant of Nebo."

[10] *Existentialism* is primarily an assortment of twentieth-century philosophies devoted to interpreting human existence in a problem-filled world.

Dialectical materialism is a philosophic approach to reality derived from the teachings of Karl Marx and Friedrich Engels. Briefly, the material world (world of objects, things, people), which can be perceived by the five senses, has its own reality, independent of the mind or the spirit. They taught that ideas were generated solely as a result of material conditions, as opposed to idealism, which taught that mind and spirit shaped ideas and matter.

Nihilism is a philosophic movement begun in nineteenth-century Russia that represents the struggle for individuality and the turning away from artificiality toward that which is useful and rational.

René Descartes, a Frenchman, in 1637 coined the term *cogito ergo sum*, which means "I think, therefore I am." Descartes contributed to philosophic thought the idea that there is a first and fundamental knowledge, which supersedes any other knowledge: the knowledge of one's self as an existing person.

Meister Eckhart (1260-1327) was a German mystic, preacher, and theologian of the Dominican Order. He was well known for his preaching and his controversial writings. At the time of his death in 1327, he had been declared a heretic by the Roman Catholic church and was appealing that decision.

Immanuel Kant was a German metaphysician and philosopher who greatly influenced succeeding philosophers with his theories of knowledge, ethics, and aesthetics. One of his most famous writings was *Critique of Pure Reason* (1781).

Jean Paul Sartre was a twentieth-century French novelist, playwright, and existentialist.

Karl Marx, a nineteenth-century thinker, political theorist, sociologist, and economist, was the architect of the modern doctrine of socialism. He and Friedrich Engels wrote *The Communist Manifesto* (1848). Marx was also the author of *Das Kapital*, an analysis of the economics of capitalism.

Martin Heidegger was a twentieth-century existentialist, a critic of technological society, and a leading ontologist (study of the nature of being and the various kinds of existence). The German word *wissenschaftlichkeit* is a philosophic term that refers to the working "scientific concept" that a philosopher applies to his or her theories.

[11] Persons in the medical profession take a Hippocratic Oath that outlines the duties of the physician to students of medicine and the duties of the pupil to the teacher. It also contains a physician's pledge to live an exemplary personal and professional life, to refrain from causing harm or hurt, and to administer only those treatments that will be beneficial to the patient.The oath is named after the ancient Greek physician Hippocrates, who is considered the father of medicine. However, the real father of medicine is the Egyptian Imhotep. For information, see footnote 1, in the sermon entitled "What Makes You So Strong?"

[12] Daniel 5

[13] Melanie Lawson, a television anchorwoman in Houston, Texas, is the daughter of Rev. William A. Lawson, pastor of Wheeler Avenue Baptist Church, where the series of sermons in this book was preached. In late 1989, she was sent to Panama by her television station to cover the events around the overthrow of the country's ruler, General Manuel Antonio Noriega.

[14] Yahweh and Miqveh are Hebrew names for God and the Messiah.

[15] Uvelingqaki and Unkulunkulu are South African names for God.

[16] Modimo and Modiri are South African names for God.

[17] Lesa (South African), ruah (Hebrew), and pneuma (Greek) all mean "spirit."

[18] For Gehazi's Judge see 2 Kings 5:20-27.

[19] For Joshua's Battleaxe see Joshua 1:5. God was Joshua's mighty weapon in battle.

[20] Jeremiah 20:9

[21] Ezekiel 1:15-28

[22] Dr. Isaac Watts (1674–1748) wrote the well-known hymn "O God, Our Help in Ages Past," which includes these lines:

"O God our help in ages past,
    Our hope for years to come."

[23] *Christology* is a term that refers to one's interpretation of the life and teachings of Jesus Christ. *Homiletics* is the art of

preaching. *Hermeneutics* is a term that refers to the way in which Scripture is interpreted. *Exegesis* is the art of drawing out of a biblical text its meaning. When one exegetes a passage of Scripture, he or she uses several methods to establish its meaning. These methods are called "biblical criticism." Several forms of criticism, including textual and literary, are used by preachers, teachers, and scholars to discern the meaning of texts. *Form criticism*, a type of biblical criticism, classifies written texts according to the forms in which they existed before they were written. Examples are parables, hymns, and poems.

What Makes You So Strong?
[1] The figure of 370 years refers to the time between 1619, when African slaves were brought to the colonies by a Dutch ship and deposited as cargo at Jamestown, and the present (*Before the Mayflower*. Lerone Bennett, Jr. New York: Penguin Books, 1966).

Imhotep, c. 2686–2613 B.C., considered a great physician, was later worshiped as the god of medicine in Egypt and Greece. He was a high executive officer, sage, astrologer, and architect, and the chief minister to Djoser, the second king of Egypt's third dynasty.

Aesop is the name traditionally given to the author of a collection of Greek fables. An Egyptian biography of the first century A.D. places him on the island of Samos as a slave who gained his freedom from his master, went to Babylon as a riddle solver to King Lycurgus, and died at Delphi.

Akhenaton, the king of Egypt (1379–1362 B.C.) of the Eighteenth Dynasty, established the worship of one god. Prior to his reign, a host of gods was worshiped in the ancient world. He taught that Aton, the sun-god was the "sole god," and not only the god of Egypt, but god of the entire creation.

Thutmose II was an Eighteenth Dynasty king of Egypt who reigned from about 1512–1504 B.C. He is best known for suppressing a revolt in Nubia, Egypt's southern territory, and for sending an expedition to Palestine to punish some rebels there. His name is found on buildings that were begun in Nubia by his father, Thutmose I, and completed during his own reign. He married his half-sister Hatshepset. His mummy, which was unrolled in 1886, is preserved in the Egyptian Museum in Cairo.

[2] Paul Robeson (1898–1976) was an African American actor, singer, and activist for the cause of freedom. A scholar, Robeson graduated with a straight *A* average from Princeton University. Like Robeson, the others mentioned here fought for freedom in their own ways: Thurgood Marshall, the first black

Supreme Court Justice, through the legal process; Malcolm X and Martin Luther King as great orators and movement leaders during the civil rights era of the 1950s and 1960s; and astronaut Ron McNair, who inspired community-based recreational programs for inner-city youth.

3 W.E.B. Dubois and Booker T. Washington were two of the most prominent African American spokesmen during the early part of this century. They represented two significant but opposite strains of thought in the life of African Americans. The intellectual Dubois was more the integrationist who believed that the "talented tenth" or top echelon in the black community should lead the masses to freedom. Washington, the first president and principal developer of Tuskegee Institute, was a practical man who favored the self-help approach of pulling one's self up by one's own bootstraps. He believed that integration would come at some future time when blacks had established themselves economically.

4 Louis Farrakhan is the leading spokesman for the Nation of Islam. The late Mickey Leland was a United States congressman from Houston, Texas. Deeply concerned about starvation in Africa, he died in 1989 in a plane crash in Ethiopia while on a mission to deliver food and supplies.

5 Younger readers may not remember Pops Staples, who was popular as a lead singer with his family, the Staples Singers, during the 1960s.

6 Luther Vandross, popular singer; Magic Johnson, former basketball player for the Los Angeles Lakers; Michael Jordan, basketball player for the Chicago Bulls; the late Harold Washington, first black mayor of Chicago; Doug Wilder, Virginia's first black governor, and the country's first black governor since Reconstruction.

7 Sterling Brown (1901–1991) one of America's leading poets, came to prominence during the great Harlem Renaissance and was known as the "dean of American poets." Vincent Harding is a noted African American historian. He is the author of *Hope and Dynasty: Why We Must Share the Story of the Movement* (Maryknoll, N.Y.: Orbis Books, 1990). Jim Forbes is the current pastor of the Riverside Church in New York City, and the church's first black pastor. Kwame Nkrumah (1908–1972) was the first prime minister of Ghana and president of the republic from the time of its independence from Great Britain in 1957 until 1966. The Reverend Allan Boesak was a leader in the Dutch Reformed Church in South Africa. Classified under the apartheid system as a "colored," he was an anti-apartheid activist who was stripped of his position in the church because of his relationship with a Caucasian woman.

William Gray is a former United States congressman (Democrat, Pennsylvania) who now heads the United Negro College
Fund. Steve Biko is a former South African activist who was
murdered in prison. *Biko,* a movie about his life, gives insights
into the struggles and agonies that faced many South African
activists. It is based on the book *Biko,* by South African jour-
nalist Donald Woods, who immortalized Steve Biko. Dave
Dinkins was the first black mayor of New York City.

8 "The Strong Men," by Sterling Brown. Reprinted from the
MASSACHUSETTS REVIEW, © 1966 The Massachusetts
Review, Inc.

9 Queen Hatshepset was the half-sister and wife of Thutmose
II. At his death she jointly reigned with his young son (Thutmose III), justifying her claim to the throne by saying that she
was a daughter of Amen-Ra, who she claimed had begotten her
in his sanctuary, and that of her two parents only her mother
was mortal. It was believed that every king of Egypt was a god
who had become incarnate through human birth of a woman.
Hatshepset was the first queen of Egypt to claim divine origin
in this way. She called herself "Khnemet Amen," a name that
indicated she was of the very essence and being and bone and
flesh of the god. In the ninth year of her reign, Hatshepset
made herself king of Egypt, and in her bas-reliefs she appears
in the form of a man, wearing male attire, the headdress of a
god, and a beard on her chin.

10 The name Candace was a title, probably meaning "queen,"
not a personal name. A number of queens from the Ethiopian
kingdom of Meroe on the Nile in modern Sudan used this title.
The Candace of Acts 8:27 apparently applied to the reigning
queen-mother, and was well known to ancient historians.

11 *Nzinga,* also known as Ana de Sousa, became the queen of
Ndongo (named Angola by the Portugese) in 1624. She pro-
tested the Portugese violations of a peace treaty with Ndongo
that had been negotiated in 1623, under her brother's rule. She
harbored fugitive slaves from Angola, welcomed into her army
Portugese-trained African soldiers, and encouraged Africans
under Portugese rule to rebel. When her stronghold was captured in 1626, she escaped to the kingdom of Matamba, which
she conquered around 1630. There she built a strong military
power base and continued her struggle to halt the Portuguese
expansion in Southern Africa.

Cleopatra VII (69–30 B.C.), the Egyptian queen made famous
by Shakespeare in his play *Julius Caesar,* was Caesar's lover
and later Mark Antony's wife. She became queen in 51 B.C.,
when her father died, ruling successively with her two brothers
and her son. When the Roman armies of Octavian defeated
their forces, she and Antony committed suicide, and Egypt

came under Roman domination. She stands out among the
women of antiquity because of her romantic appeal, great
beauty, and driving ambition.
Nefertiti was the queen of Egypt from 1379–1362 B.C. The wife
of Akhenaton, she supported his religious revolution, which replaced many gods with the sun-god, Aton. She bore six daughters, two of whom became queens. Her famous portrait bust of
painted limestone, now in a museum in Germany, was found at
Tell el-Amarna.
Makeda, the queen of Sheba, ruled in the tenth century B.C.
The Old Testament records her visit to King Solomon to test
his world-renowned wisdom by asking him to solve riddles. She
came with gifts of gold, jewels, and spices. According to Ethiopian tradition, she and Solomon married, and their son, Mene-
lik I, founded the royal dynasty of Ethiopia.
Hadassah is the Hebrew name for Esther in the Book of Esther.
[12] Angela Davis is a Communist party activist of the 1960s and
1970s, who became a professor. Toni Morrison is a Pulitzer
Prize winning novelist, well known for such novels as *Song of
Solomon* and *Beloved*. Barbara Jordan is a great orator and
well-known former congresswoman from Texas. She was con-
firmed as one of the country's most articulate and capable orators during her dynamic speech at the Democratic National
Convention in 1976. Betty Shabazz is the widow of Malcolm X
and an activist in her own right. Oprah Winfrey is the highest-
paid and most popular television talk show host and producer
of her own show. Winnie Mandela, South African freedom
fighter, is the former wife of Nelson Mandela, head of the African National Congress.
[13] Nannie Helen Burroughs (1879–1961) was an outstanding orator and outspoken spokeswoman for Christianity and wom-
en's and civil rights. She was a staunch Baptist, having
founded the Women's Convention (later called the Women's
Auxiliary) of the National Baptist Convention, U.S.A. She was
the corresponding secretary of this group from 1900 to 1947,
and its president from 1948 to 1961. Dr. Burroughs founded
the National Training School for Women in 1901. It was located
in Washington, D.C., and is now an elementary school bearing
her name. Under her leadership, the NBC Women's Auxiliary
created *The Worker*, a mission periodical, which is still widely
used by church missions circles. Fannie Lou Hamer, an outspoken freedom fighter from Ruleville, Mississippi, was one of
two representatives seated from the sixty-member Mississippi
Freedom Democratic Party that traveled to the 1964 Democratic National Convention. She and her husband lost their
jobs and risked their lives to register to vote in Mississippi.

Jessie "Ma" Houston led a most effective prison ministry in the 1970s and 1980s.

[14] Roberta Flack, Anita Baker, and Nina Simone represent three generations of song stylists whose songs have contained positive messages. Jackie Joyner-Kersee is an Olympic track star.

[15] Rebecca Lee, the first African American woman to graduate from medical school, finished at the New England Female Medical College in 1864.

[16] Reverends Jini Moore (now Jini Ross), Gwenn Pierre, Barbara Williams, Lola Nelson, Devanah Johns, Lana Reese, LaVerne Harris, and Mickey Moseley were all ministers at the Wheeler Avenue Baptist Church in Houston in 1990, when I preached this sermon there. Rev. Joan Campbell was moderator of the Presbyterian Church (USA), and Bishop Barbara Harris is the first woman bishop in the Episcopal church.

[17] Melanie Lawson is a television news anchor for the ABC affiliate station in Houston. She is the daughter of Rev. William A. Lawson, pastor of Houston's Wheeler Avenue Baptist Church.

[18] Zora Neal Hurston (1903–1960) was a black folklorist and writer during the Harlem Renaissance. She is best known for her second novel, published in 1937, *Their Eyes Were Watching God*. Mari Evans is a poet who emerged during the 1960s, when there was a second "renaissance" in black arts. Mary Se Conde is the author of *Segu* and *The Children of Segu*. Gladys Knight, popular singer, gained fame singing in the 1960s in the singing group Gladys Knight and the Pips.

[19] Zimbabwe, Angola, and Namibia are Southern African countries that fought for and gained independence. Women were notably part of the armed forces in these struggles. Soweto is a township in South Africa where students rebelled in the 1970s when the government tried to impose certain educational reforms, among them making the Afrikaaner (Dutch-based) language their official language.

[20] Cheops, Greek for the Egyptian name Khufu, was the second king of the Fourth Dynasty of Egypt (c. 2613–2494 B.C.) and the builder of the Great Pyramid at Giza, the largest single building that had ever been built. Maat was the Egyptian goddess of order, law, right, truth, and wisdom. The lodge is in her name.

[21] Jesse Owens (1913–1980) was a United States track and field athlete, who set a world record in the running broad jump that stood for twenty-five years. He won four gold medals in the 1936 Olympic Games in Berlin, upsetting Adolf Hitler's plan to use the games to demonstrate Aryan superiority.

[22] Dr. Jawanza Kunjufu is a consultant on the education of Af-

rican American youth and the author of a number of books, including volumes one and two of *Countering the Conspiracy to Destroy Black Boys* (Chicago: African American Images, 1985, 1986).

[23] David Goldstine, et al,*The Dance-Away Lover: And Other Roles We Play in Love, Sex, and Marriage* (New York: Morrow, 1977).

[24] A person who took a Nazirite vow could do so for a consecrated period of time or for a lifetime. Samuel was a lifelong Nazirite (1 Samuel 1:11), and apparently so was Samson. The vow was marked by letting one's hair grow and abstaining from wine and strong drinks. "Nazirite" means "one consecrated, devoted, separated." Historically the Nazirite was a sacred person.

[25] Judges 13:1-6

[26] Dr. Carter G. Woodson (1875–1950) was a historian who emphasized the importance of the history of African Americans. He founded the Association for the Study of Negro Life and History in 1915, and edited the first issue of the association's principal scholarly publication, *The Journal of Negro History*. In 1926 he founded Negro History Week. Dr. Bobby Wright is an eminent psychologist who taught at the University of Chicago.

[27] Dagon (Hebrew for Dagan) was a west semitic god of corn, but was confused by the Israelites with the Hebrew "dag," meaning fish. The visual image of Dagon was of a fish-tailed being. Dagon appears in the Old Testament as the chief god of the Philistines (Judges 16:23).

[28] Senator Edward Brooke (Republican, Massachusetts) was the first black United States senator, elected in 1966. In 1978, following his divorce, he lost his bid for a third term because of "conduct unbecoming a senator," meaning the way he treated his wife, who was white. Conversely, Senator Ted Kennedy, who led the attack on Brooke, went scot-free after his involvement in the death of Mary Jo Kopechne. Ms. Kopechne was Kennedy's companion one night in 1969, when he accidentally drove his car off an unmarked bridge on Chappaquidick Island, near Martha's Vineyard, Massachusetts. She was drowned. He was found guilty of leaving the scene of an accident, but was reelected to the Senate in 1970.

[29] Judges 13:25, GNB

[30] Psalm 46:1, KJV

[31] Isaiah 40:29, KJV

[32] Dr. King attended graduate school at Boston University, and Crozer Theological Seminary.

[33] My doctoral dissertation is on the African American music

tradition. For twenty-four years my field of study has been our music, including the music of the Caribbean and of South America. I've come to love all of our music, and when I hear our worship services murdered with dead music, I don't feel like preaching. I'm just too mad to preach. This argument in our churches over types of music is nothing new. It goes way back to the 1700s when the A.M.E. church pulled out of St. George's Methodist Episcopal Church in Philadelphia. The new A.M.E. church was in part composed of well-to-do West Indians who thought that the only worthy sacred music was British music. Many African American musicians have been trained that way. They will only use British and European music in services. In the mid-nineteenth century, Bishop Alexander Payne of the A.M.E. church in Charleston, South Carolina, took issue with his people who wanted their tambourines, rhythms, and beats. He said this music was an abomination. One of the old presiding elders from Africa told Bishop Payne that without the beat "the Spirit don't come."